FRANKSTOWN: ANATOMY OF AN AMBUSH

by

Roger G. Swartz, M.A. Ed., M.P.A.

Illustrated by
Karen L. Pennebaker

BLUE PATH PRESS
Hockessin, Delaware

1995

Copyright 1995, Roger G. Swartz
R.G. Swartz & Associates
All rights reserved. No portion of this book may be utilized,
disseminated and/or electronically stored and retreived
in any manner without prior written permission of the author.

Direct orders to:
R.G. Swartz & Associates
Telephone: 717-299-5061 FAX: 717-560-0522

ISBN: 1-887109-01-3
Library of Congress Catalog Card Number: 95-76319

First edition
Published in the United States of America

DEDICATION

This work is dedicated to:

William W. Hummel,
Professor Emeritus of History, Albright College
(Reading, PA), who first guided me to the rangers,
taught me critical thinking skills of the historian,
and from whom I have learned.

ACKNOWLEDGEMENTS

I want to thank those who shared with me the creation of this manuscript. Robert Emerson, Executive Director of the Railroad Museum of Pennsylvania, served as my mentor and shared his expertise regarding both the immediate events surrounding the ambush at Frankstown and his knowledge of Revolutionary War historic sites in Blair County, PA. Many relaxing hours have been spent with Mr. Emerson discussing the rangers, French & Indian and Revolutionary Wars on Pennsylvania's frontiers; and, concerning the ambush at Frankstown, the exact location of the raiding party's base camp.

I am grateful to Margaret Goodman, Executive Director, Fort Roberdeau Historic Site (Altoona, PA) and the Fort Roberdeau Association, who initiated this research project. Holly Stuttler, of Elaine Ainsworth & Associates, gave invaluable aid in the typing of the original manuscript. Brent Burket of Lancaster, PA, served as proofreader. Karen Pennebaker of R.G. Swartz & Associates has served as illustrator, format and layout editor, typist in amendments to the manuscript, and as editor. Margaret Goodman gave this project life. The latter three have nourished and sustained it.

Paula Zitzler, archaeologist, contributed to the editing and gave me new sources concerning both archaeology and culture of the Iroquois. Trish Spath, ("Sweet Voice Woman") of Onondaga Iroquois lineage, contributed to the editing of Section 4, "People of the Long House", and to the author's knowledge and understanding of Iroquoian culture and rituals.

Others kept me on this journey at critical times, leading to this work's inception. Thomas Clegg, President of the Muncy Historical Society (Muncy, PA) gave this work its original impetus through his inviting me to give a presentation to the Society about ranging companies. Jane Jackson, Editor of *Now and Then* (Magazine of the Muncy Historical Society), requested of me an article concerning the rangers. These requests spurred further research. Josephine Isenberg, staff member of the Fort Roberdeau Historic Site, presented my first *Now and Then* article to the Executive Director of this site.

Finally, I wish to thank the many researchers from libraries in this country and Canada who have greatly enhanced my knowledge base and have gone "the extra mile" to expedite my obtaining primary source material. Special thanks go to the Special Collections Room of the Ganser Library of Millersville University; the Public Archives of Canada; the Wisconsin Historical Society; and the library of the Northumberland County Historical Society (Fort Augusta Museum, Sunbury, PA). Charlotte Walker, of the latter, has provided me with invaluable help. Many of the volumes of the Works Progress Administration Journals, located here, contain valuable resources involving Central Pennsylvania Revolutionary War history

                                                        Roger Swartz
                                                       April 1995

ILLUSTRATIONS

Figure 2.1. Assunepachla..	4
Frontier cabin...	7
Indian women at work..	14
Figure 4.1. Boundary Line of the 1768 Treaty of Fort Stanwix	20
Figure 4.2. Fort Stanwix Treaty Line............................	21
British rangers..	34
Pennsylvania militia...	47
Figure 6.1. Counties of Pennsylvania...........................	48
Figure 7.1. Breech Clout & Leggings...........................	64
Figure 7.2. Pennsylvania Ranger Recruitment Oath - 1780	70
Indian encampment..	76
Warrior...	79
Figure 10.1. The Frankstown Path................................	80
Figure 10.2. Ambush at Frankstown, June 3, 1781......	84

The artist who illustrated this publication, Karen Pennebaker, is the Format and Layout Editor of R.G. Swartz & Associates. A graduate of Penn State, she exhibits paintings and block prints, teaches children's art classes and spends a lot of time in front of a computer screen. This book was designed in LotusWorks on a Packard Bell 386 computer and typeset on a Hewlett Packard LaserJet 2P+ printer.

TABLE OF CONTENTS

Introduction..	viii
Section 1: Beginnings: Planting the Seeds...........................	1
Section 2: Assunepachla: Frankstown's Roots.....................	5
Section 3: By Axe, Plow and Sword...................................	8
Section 4: People of the Long House (Frankstown Combatants).................................	15
Section 5: Butler's Rangers: Winged Retribution (Frankstown Combatants).................................	35
Section 6: Pennsylvania Militia: Sword or Plow? (Frankstown Combatants).................................	49
Section 7: Pennsylvania Rangers: Traces of Honor (Frankstown Combatants).................................	57
Section 8: Prelude to an Ambush (Patriot Forces)...............	71
Section 9: Prelude to an Ambush (Tory Forces)..................	77
Section 10: We Who Stood, We Who Fell...........................	81
Section 11: Aftermath...	93
Conclusion..	99
Footnotes: Section 1...	101
Section 2...	105
Section 3...	106
Section 4...	108
Section 5...	116
Section 6...	121
Section 7...	123
Section 8...	129
Section 9...	131
Section 10...	134
Section 11...	137
Bibliography:..	141
Biographical Information faces back cover.	

Introduction

Anatomy can be either the study of the soma (the physical body) or of a body of work. The body of work herein represents the ambush at Frankstown (south of present-day Altoona and west of Hollidaysburg) that occurred early Sunday morning, June 3, 1781. It involved four principal forces that often met on the Pennsylvania frontier. These were: the Pennsylvania rangers and militia, who were primarily responsible for frontier defense; and Butler's Rangers and their Iroquoian allies, who were responsible for implementing British war strategy as it concerned the frontiers.

British war strategy had three major goals:
- * Destroy the granaries that fed the Rebel armies
- * Siphon men from Washington's eastern theatre of war operations, giving the Rebels two theatres of war with which to contend, thereby weakening them
- * Obtain food and supplies for British western troops and Indian allies

The study of anatomy can focus in two directions. On the one hand, it is a detailed, minute analysis of a specific body part. This has been the primary focus in allopathic (western) medicine. On the other hand, it is the study of the interrelationships of parts. For want of a better term, this is called holistic medicine. As an example of the latter approach, the body's immune system consists of, among other things, neurotransmitters which communicate with various types of cells in the immune system. These key cells in turn combat foreign bacteria. The neurotransmitters "travel" through the soma and are also produced by the brain's limbic system and major organs of the body. Thus the body is a web of life in this holistic view. Touch one strand of the web and the whole web vibrates.

In the analytical direction of anatomy, minute, detailed analysis is used. Parts are studied in isolation from one another. Such analysis applied to Frankstown reveals an isolated event long since forgotten in the backwash of history, except by local historians and genealogists researching their ancestors. There is a very thin line between doing isolated analysis and inadvertently choosing sides, losing perspective - and facts. In the analytical direction of "anatomical" history, it easily becomes "us" against "them": the barbarian savages infesting the frontiers is one phrase uncovered by this author in more than one 19th century historian. In this case, the Indian becomes the savage bacteria, infesting the healthy body. Detailed analysis by an historian can lead to loss of perspective, leading to loss of facts, leading to myth as history. Both myth and history have energy, but myth is not history.

Analysis does have one major advantage: An objective, detailed, thorough study can lead to uncovering new data, especially if rigorous attempt is made to corroborate the facts. Western medicine is indeed scientific in its approach. Such an investigation applied to the history of Frankstown reveals two different lists of men serving: the PA ranger and the militia. In the past, historians studying Frankstown have listed most of the men who actually served, but either called them militia or rangers. Further research, listed in this book, finds that both types of military units were present, and itemized each man in terms of the type of military unit in which he served.

Given this analysis, it then becomes imperative for the historian studying Frankstown to become a military historian: How do two independent units, who were not used to fighting together, function in time of crisis? Especially when their enemy has fought together for almost four years already? And who is the enemy? A fundamental axiom: never underestimate the enemy's strength or their skill level. Boyd's Rangers and voluntary militia that early morning of June 3rd were up against two of the best fighting units ever on the North American continent: the Iroquois warrior and the British Loyalist ranger.

Approaching history as "holistic anatomy" leads to uncovering facts heretofore unknown regarding Frankstown. Some of these are:

* PA rangers were not militia. They had their own duties, functions, structures and organization. These Revolutionary War military units have largely been unrecognized in the state of Pennsylvania. Ranging companies existed prior to 1779. However, the events in this text encompass 1779 on and lay the necessary background for the ambush at Frankstown.

* Butler's Rangers (British Loyalist rangers) served at Frankstown. Their battle tactics were manifest at Frankstown.
* A cursory examination of the Iroquoian culture reveals a sense of the Native American war tactics and how and why they were employed June 3, 1781.
* The preliminaries and the aftermath of combat are part of the intricate web of history. This book reveals some of the salient facts (including Native American and Euro-American frontier society) and what happened to some of the prisoners.

In this holistic view of history, Frankstown serves as a case study to what often happened on Pennsylvania's frontiers when these four units met in combat. Facts lead to understanding. To understand Frankstown and Revolutionary War frontier history, the lay reader as well as the professional historian must understand the four types of military units who fought there.

In attempting to develop this understanding, it is very difficult to develop an 18th century Euro-American mind-set. Technology becomes not a match, but flint and steel. Skills become not how to load computer software but how to load and fire a long rifle.

It is harder yet, in developing this understanding, to leap from the 20th century into an 18th century Native American mind-set. Can you, the reader, understand the importance of ritual in making the transition from a "peace mode" to a "war mode" and back again? Can you understand the importance of not mixing ("infecting" would also fit here) female energy with male energy before, during, and after a raid? Of the primary importance of mourning losses over accomplishment of additional military objectives? Can you truly understand the importance of clan and community rather than individual ownership of land? All these concepts and many more were played out at Frankstown.

This introduction to the Iroquois is but an orientation, focused upon a limited, set time span: the American Revolution, from Lexington and Concord in 1775 through 1782, the last year of major fighting on the frontiers. This is an important time. Iroquois culture is in a rapid state of flux, their population decimated by European contact through war and disease; their old culture forever maimed by European contact: loss of land, depletion of population leading to a need for but a dearth of leadership; and, reliance upon European trade goods and alcohol. (European trade goods, as represented by the abundant British storehouse, were a major reason why the Iroquois sided with Britain in the American Revolution.) Yet they are attempting to preserve "the old ways". Within this difficult setting, I attempt to portray the Iroquois and their culture, hopefully giving you some understanding of their actions before, during and after the Frankstown ambush.

Some of these actions may be stated in the main body's narrative. But when I felt it would impede the flow of the narrative, they appear as supplemental material within footnotes. This applies not only to Section 4, "People of the Long House", but to other subject content as well. The reader is encouraged to read and study these footnotes as much as the main subject content. These footnotes contain new source material which correct past historical inaccuracies. I apologize for their length but I felt it important to disseminate this new information.

The reader is encouraged to turn to the Bibliography for further elaboration. Finally, for experiential learning, he is encouraged to explore the historic interpretative sites located in Pennsylvania and New York.

Other elaborative notes need to be made: I have purposefully used "he" in this introduction and in the text in place of he/she, him/her, etc., in order to keep the narrative flowing. Some of the words in italics are given to help the reader get an experiential feel for this time period. As such, it is placed in the language and context of the times - not necessarily reflecting the values of myself as author. Some of the quotations used in speech are also representative and furthermore do not reflect a direct quote from another copyrighted source. When copying directly from a manuscript in the public domain, the work is cited via footnotes; the wording and spelling are kept to the original. Words in brackets included in manuscript text are merely for modern interpretation.

In writing this manuscript, I have substantially used historical, anthropological and archaelogical sources. However, know and understand that I am a white male from the late 20th century. Certainly, I have my own filters which distort my perspective. Given this, I have attempted to be objective.

                Roger Swartz
                January, 1995

Section 1:

Beginnings: Planting the Seeds

1781. Spring came early this year to the land, earlier than last spring.

The winter of 1779-1780 was one of the severest in the history of North America. In the spring of last year, settlers in the Schoharie settlements of New York were tapping sugar maple on snowshoes.[1] That winter:
- Deer and other animals perished in large numbers. [2]
- The Detroit River was entirely frozen over - an unheard-of natural event.
- At Detroit, drifts were approximately ten feet high. [3] In York Town (New York), held by the British Army and Tory (Loyalist) Forces, snow began falling in November and continued almost unabated to the middle of March, 1780. By spring, York Island (Manhattan) was forever stripped of wood - deforested - for the burning of firewood. With the ice, boat transportation of wood and provisions was nonexistent. The city was isolated. All shacks, fences, even ships were cut down for firewood. Many froze to death. [4]
- The Niagara River was frozen over for two continuous months, also unheard of. [5]
- About Fort Niagara, newspapers were reporting hundreds of Iroquois dying of starvation, [6] hypothermia, and perhaps scurvy. [7]
- The Allegheny Mountain gaps held 8-10 feet of snow. [8]
- In addition to the Niagara, the major rivers traversing the land, including the Ohio, Susquehanna, Delaware, Mississippi and the Potomac, were frozen over. [9]

This, of course, held true for the St. Lawrence, the major supply artery for all of Britain's Canadian and northwestern forts. Normally, the British government in Canada had to have on hand six months of advance supplies for its settlers, citizens, traders and military garrisons such as Detroit, Michilimackinac, and Niagara. Niagara serviced these former posts. [10]

The Iroquois Confederacy was devastated that previous summer (1779) by the Sulllivan Expedition. General John Sullivan's army, numbering over 4500 men [11] had, by its return to Tioga Point (Athens, PA) on September 29, 1779, [12] achieved these results: [13]
> * Destroyed 40 towns of the Iroquois Confederacy.
> * Destroyed over 160,000 bushels of corn (with ears measuring 22 inches in length and cornstalks measuring 16 feet high.
> * Cut down all orchards of these towns (one orchard had 1500 trees).
> * Destroyed numerous other vegetable crops growing in abundance: beans, potatoes, squash, pumpkins, cucumbers, watermelons.
> * So displaced the Iroquois Confederacy, that by the winter of 1779-1780, more than 2600 Iroquois were living in temporary quarters about Fort Niagara.

This swath of destruction was akin to Sherman's "March through Georgia" and the pillaging of the Shenandoah granaries by Sheridan during the Civil War. This added greatly to the expense of the war for Great Britain, and threatened the fur trade - a major, if not the major, source of revenue from the New World. Sir Frederick Haldimand (governor of Canada), by November 1779, had dispatched numerous critical and pressing letters to the Secretary of War for the Colonies, stressing that if the fur trade was to be saved, a solution had to be found for provisioning the Northwest parts - aside from the regular six months' inability to supply the parts due to inclement weather. [14]

Thus Niagara was not a self-sufficient fort by the time the Iroquois were driven to it. It was not until the spring of 1780 that an agricultural plan proposed by Governor Haldimand was implemented at Niagara, [15] with the Iroquois, under one of their principal war chiefs, Joseph Brant (of the Mohawk Nation), planting and producing the first crop - corn.

To keep perspective, 1780 was the fifth year of the commencement of hostilities, since the events at Concord and Lexington in the spring of 1775. Even by September of 1781, Governor Haldimand could still write that the

Rangers (Butler's Rangers - see Section 5) were within a few days of evacuating Niagara due to lack or provisions. [16]

This displacement involved more than the Indians. It also included loyalists from New York originally living in the Mohawk and Hudson River valleys, Northern Pennsylvania at Tioga Point, and those loyalists living in settlements about the headwaters of the North Branch of the Susquehanna and the Delaware Rivers. The latter settlements were located in areas such as the Schohaire and Cherry Valley. These, too, were driven in upon Niagara, blown by the whirlwind of Sullivan's march of destruction. This exodus to Niagara had begun prior to Sullivan's expedition; Sullivan accelerated it. Thus, Niagara became a beacon, a rallying point for resistance by the king's men. This movement further aggravated the problem of the already-short supplies on hand. [17]

The eighteenth century Shawnees called February "the Hunger Moon." [18] This savage winter, this fourth winter of the war, saw cold, stark famine etched in her face.

The Sullivan Expedition had two more results:
* British and Indian tactics were changed forever more, due to greater travel distances to reach the settlements.
* In this particular Hunger Moon, the seeds of revenge were planted deep.

Figure 2.1. Assunepachla.

Section 2:
Assunepachla: Frankstown's Roots

Assunepachla is the Indian name for Frankstown. (See Figure 2.1 for illustration of Delaware village.) Jones [1] states that it signifies "a meeting of many waters" or "where the waters join". That meaning is possible, considering where the Indian village stood: at the south side of the Frankstown Branch of the Juniata River, opposite the mouth of the Beaverdam Branch and at the mouth of Oldtown Run (see Figure 10.1, Section 10). [2]

Assunepachla, according to Donehoo, might also signify "Stone Valley". It was an Indian village of Delaware peoples (Lenni Lenape was the proper name for these peoples). [3] Jones states upon the advance of Forbes' army in 1758, during the last great French and Indian war, the village was finally abandoned. [4] At the commencement of hostilities, the warriors of this village took up the war belt offered by the French and went to the Ohio country. In this war, many Delawares sided with the French.

This village was on the Frankstown Indian Path, connecting Harris' Ferry (Harrisburg) with the Indian village of Kittanning (the present-day Kittanning), another Delaware village by the outbreak of the French and Indian War. Part of the Frankstown Path is illustrated in Figure 10.1, Section 10. Up until the American Revolution, this was the preferred route of Pennsylvania Indian traders taking pack trains into the Ohio country. Another path from Kittanning lead to the Forks of the Ohio (Pittsburgh). The Frankstown Path west from Hollidaysburg was called the Kittanning Path, the name used locally by historians to this day. After the French and Indian War, traffic was increased upon the Forbes Road to the south, a military road following the Raystown Path. (See Wallace, *Indian Paths of Pennsylvania*, Bibliography.)

One cannot begin to understand the nature of the Revolution on Pennsylvania's frontiers during the American Revolution without a knowledge of geography, Indian paths and Indian history. As flowed the waters, so flowed the events of history. Where there were waters, there were Indian villages. Where existed Indian villages, existed trader goods. Traders followed the paths to reach the villages. Traders dealt in more than commerce. They were the progenitors of settlement. Many, such as Pennsylvania's George Croghan, were also land speculators. Indeed, George Croghan was Deputy Superintendent of Indian Affairs, Northern District, Indian Department, under the jurisdiction of the Colonial Secretary, Great Britain. His immediate supervisor was William Johnson, Superintendent of Indian Affairs, residing at Johnson Hall (near Johnstown, NY). It was control of Indian trade in the Ohio country that lead to the final war between Great Britain and France for control of North America. Croghan was a close friend of Johnson, and the father-in-law of Joseph Brant, the Mohawk (Iroquois) war chief.

John Hart and Frank Stevens also were such traders. The Frankstown District, comprising many present townships of Bedford County, was named after Frank Stevens. Historians have stated that it was named after a German trader called Stephen (or Steven) Frank, but no information is available on this man. That is because of an error in the records. Stephen (or Steven) Frank never existed. As Donehoo states, citing as his source the PA Archives (First Series, vol. 2, 136) [5] that in a table of distances given by one John Harris, he (Harris) lists the distance to "Frank's (Stephen's) Town - 5 miles". An incorrect apostrophe was placed in the table. There should have been no apostrophe in "Stephen's". Donehoo further states that while there is no record of Stephen (or Steven) Frank as a trader, Frank Stevens was a prominent trader. Thus the district was named after his (Frank Stevens) first name.

There were conspicuous locations along the Frankstown Path. Two were named after John Hart, another trader. Hart's Log became, by the time of the Revolution, a Bedford County settlement (present-day Alexandria). It was so named because Hart had hollowed out a log for a trough to water horses. [6] Approximately 16 miles to the west of Hollidaysburg was a camp site, Hart's Sleeping Place. Since there were two Indian traders by the same name, John Hart, [7] it cannot be ascertained by this writer which is specifically associated with which site(s). Another location was Water Street, so named because trader pack trains used the stream bed for passage through the narrow gap in Tussey Mountain. [8]

By the Revolution, Hart's Log, Water Street and the Frankstown District were prominent clusters of settlement in Bedford County, [9] created as a political jurisdiction in the colony of Pennsylvania in March, 1771. [10]

Primitive frontier cabin with smokehole in roof.

Notes:

Section 3:
By Axe, Plow and Sword

The Frankstown District was settled by Scotch-Irish and a few Germans, following the traders. On Assunepachla and the river's flats, the remains of Indian huts were replaced by the cabin and clearings. American Indians believed everything had soul and spirit. [1] If so, the forest trembled, for itself heard the sharp thunk of the axe, felt itself shudder, and saw itself transformed.

Contrary to popular myths, the log cabin is not the time worn founding symbol of the 13 colonies. The Swedes and Germans of the fur trading colony of New Sweden (founded at the mouth of the Delaware River in 1636) introduced the log dwelling house to the American colonies. The colonists of Jamestown used wattle and daub; the Plymouth Pilgrims used the oak frame sheathed with weatherboard (now called clapboard). The Scotch-Irish, arriving in large numbers after 1718, were the first English speaking colonists to adopt it. [2]

Using axes, a few workmen could lay open a "clearing" (approximately 1/8 acre), keeping the center beyond the reach of falling trees, and create a log "house". This was a temporary dwelling, small with low walls of round logs and slanting roof to shed rain and snow. The roofs consisted of black ash or elm bark, 2 feet wide in 4 foot lengths. The rough side, the bark, was what faced the elements. A hole cut in this roof allowed smoke to escape from a fire built on the earth floor. Construction generally followed this pattern: base logs were set upon flat rocks; walls were of notched logs to the minimum height; poles set up in position for rafters; the roof placed upon the top, with poles or small timbers used to flatten out the strips used for the roof; a hole cut in the roof for the fire built on the earth floor. Cracks between the logs were chinked with either wood wedges, moss, or clay. In place of a door, the entranceway hung with a heavy blanket or quilt. [3]

In such temporary quarters the settler passed the first winter. By the second spring and summer, with the first planting and harvesting in his clearing, the settler would have made "improvements" in his land. Such improvements would see the erection of a permanent shelter: a log cabin with floor, fireplace and chimney. The first chimneys and fireplaces were built either with stone or by wood and sticks, later replaced by stone. [4] Beneath the floor was a "root cellar" for the storage of fruits and vegetable roots. [5] This aforementioned initial cabin would be turned into a barn.

Clearing the land for plowing was an arduous task. A good chopper could clear an acre and pile brush in a week. Three men with oxen could fell an acre in a day. Hence, another myth: that of the "rugged individualist". The frontiersman was interdependent upon others from day one. The Scots soon learned to fell living trees parallel to facilitate logging. Logs cut in 15 foot lengths were drug by oxen, rolled into piles, and burnt. From this derived potash, a product which had a constant demand in England, for use in manufacture of soap and glass. Ashes from such burnt piles of logs were taken to an established ashery in the settled "interior" (that land nearest the eastern coasts). In Cherry Valley, NY, such ashes brought 7-8 pence per bushel. 450 bushels would make a ton of potash. [6]

The crops planted in the clearings the second spring upon the land were corn and wheat. Corn was grown in the flat lands, along the streams and river banks. This black earth was too rich for wheat, which thrived on knolls. The settler rarely tilled the land for the first crop, but only raked the ground as clean as possible, sowed the wheat and covered it either by harrowing or drawing a bush over it. [7] Before sowing, over rough land, with tree stumps and boulders, only ploughs drawn by 1-2 draught animals could be used. Hence an early importance of the blacksmith: to keep plows sharpened. [8]

Corn was the staple crop. Scots learned from the Indians that "roasting ears" could be boiled and eaten with drawn butter. Cornmeal could be cooked as mush, combined with meat, or mixed with water, laid on a board before the fire to bake, and eaten hot. Combined with eggs and milk, it produced "johnnycake". Dried corn was soaked in a weak lye solution to remove the hulls, and to obtain hominy - the kernel of the corn. Corn was dried in the open air, through the Indian-devised husking peg and the slatted crib. Hominy (the corn kernel) was pounded fine in wood or stone mortars, parched, and mixed with maple sugar. This served as food during travel. Another food used in travel was dried cornmeal (ground corn grain after roasting) mixed with water. 1/4 pint of cornmeal was mixed with a pint of boiling water. The Indian succotash consisted of green corn, beans and squash (the traditional "three sisters") and the fat meat of dog. White settlers substituted pork for dog and omitted the squash. The stalks and blades of corn were stacked and became cattle's fodder. [9]

Cattle also fed upon the tops of maple and linden (basswood) trees which were felled constantly for this use. We are familiar with the modern psychological Pavlovian conditioning response: ring a bell and the dog salivates. Then, on the frontiers, fell a tree and the cattle scampered toward the sound. Cattle roamed free, as did the settlers' hogs, which were fond of hunting rattlesnakes. [10]

The hogs were more agile than modern varieties and could leap a rail fence, the Scots' first farm enclosures. Sheep were kept in pens at night, enclosures resembling the foundation of the first cabins (see above) to guard against wolves, wildcats (bobcats) and "painters" (panthers: the mountain lion). [11]

In the spring, an important event for the settler was the harvesting of wool. In late May, sheep were shorn. The fleece was separated into quality. Women used the finest fleece for stockings; the next best for men's clothing; and the roughest for blankets. The spinning wheel was used to spin the wool into yarn. [12]

A farm as described above, consisting of improved buildings and clearings, was called a plantation.

The above descriptions fit both the New York and Pennsylvania frontier. In both colonies, settlement followed the trader and the military road. In both colonies, the sword was co-dependent with the plow and the axe. The land needed to be cleared, and it needed to be held permanently. Hence forts.

Military forts attracted settlers. Four examples of erected military forts

emanating from military expeditions and settlements springing up from the cleared forest about them include, from the French and Indian War and Pontiac's Conspiracy (1755-1763), in Pennsylvania:
* Fort Augusta (Sunbury)
* Forts Dusquesne (French) and Pitt (British) (Pittsburgh)
* Fort Bedford (Bedford)
* Fort Ligonier (Ligonier)

During warfare, settlers needed places offering protection. Clustering near each other, creating communities of interdependent needs, settlers would also build forts or petition the colony for such, thereby creating common places of protection and/or common rallying places for the militia. In the French and Indian War, 1755-1763 (including Pontiac's Conspiracy of 1763), Pennsylvania as a colony built forts spanning the Appalachians. These could be as elaborate as Fort Augusta (Sunbury), with bastions and cannon, or stockaded blockhouses. Individual settlers would also fortify their homes or construct blockhouses upon their farms: two story log shelters with the top portion overhanging the lower and chinked with loopholes for rifle and musket fire. Settlers might also stockade their homes.

As in the French and Indian War, so also in the Revolution. During the Revolution, an active verb form came into being, called "forting": living within the fort until either the fort capitulated in time of attack or until the danger passed.

To the west were mountains, the Allegheny mountains. Common points of invasion through these seemed to be Conemaugh (currently Johnstown), the gap at Frankstown, and the Lead Mine Gap. [13] Within the Frankstown District, now in Blair County, but then a part of Bedford County, several forts came into existence for such protection. William Holliday constructed a blockhouse on his farm southwest of the present Hollidaysburg. His brother, Adam Holliday, was instrumental in helping Peter Titus convert his barn into a fort. Titus' Fort was called Fort Holliday and was situated approximately one mile southeast of the present Hollidaysburg (south of the river) and slightly southeast of William Holliday's residence (south of the river). [14] Facing west, near Holliday's fortified house, was Fort Fetter, approximately west of Hollidaysburg and northwest of Holliday's. [15] Montgomery states that Fort

Fetter was a blockhouse; [16] Jones that it was a stockade, [17] and garrisoned by as many as 25 men, having been built in 1777. [18]

Also within Blair County, in Sinking Valley, General Roberdeau had, with his own money, constructed Fort Roberdeau for the protection of the lead miners. [19] Just north of Fort Roberdeau, in the same valley, was Fort Roller, a fort developed by Jacob Roller for the protection of his family and neighbors. [20] In Canoe Valley, which may or may not have been considered part of the Frankstown district, stood Fort Lowrey, a blockhouse built in the winter of 1778 or 1779, situated approximately three miles southwest of Water Street, in present-day Catharine Township, Blair County. It, too, was a private fort, erected for the defense of the local settlers. [21] The fort was built either by Daniel or Lazarus Lowrey, Indian traders as early as 1740, on the land initially owned by Daniel or Lazarus. [22]

Near Fort Fetter (to the northwest) was eventually built what was called the Frankstown Blockhouse. [23] It was this blockhouse, also known as Fort Fetter, that was to play a prominent role in the events of Sunday, June 3, 1781, in the ambush. (Figures 10.1 and 10.2., Section 10, illustrate the locations of Titus'; William Holliday's fortified house; Fort Fetter; and the Frankstown Blockhouse.)

Indian women at work.

Section 4:
People of the Long House
(Frankstown Combatants)

"Iroquoia" was the nation state of the Iroquois, consisting of a league, or confederacy, of five separate nations. The League, as it was formally known, was the result of centuries of war and negotiation and may have been formed as early as 1390. [1] It certainly was in place by at least the end of the 1500's, as suggested by archeological data. [2] This confederation was developed within the present day boundaries of the state of New York *in situ,* meaning in place. Archaeologists believe that the Iroquois had not migrated from other regions in North America while this confederation was developing. Hence the term, *in situ.* [3]

The league originally consisted of five separate nations. These were, from eastern to western New York: [4]

* Mohawk
* Oneida
* Onondaga
* Cayuga
* Seneca

After defeat by the North Carolina colonists in 1713, the Tuscarora Nation searched for new homelands. The Iroquoian League allowed them to settle in Iroquoia and, by the beginning of the Revolution, they were admitted as the sixth member of the League. After their adoption, the League became known as the Six Nations. [5]

Other Native American groups, notably the Delaware (the Leni Lanape: "original people"), were also under the protection of the confederation throughout the mid-18th century to the American Revolution, though they never were formally given membership status to the League. [6]

During the 17th century, the Iroquois Confederacy had fought diverse Native American nations over control of the fur trade. Iroquoian homelands in present New York state were becoming depleted of beaver after about 1640. [7] The Beaver Wars, as this era of Iroquoian history has been named, allowed them to compensate for lack of supply by becoming, in the parlance of the 20th century, "middlemen" in the fur trade. The League subjugated various other Native American nations in these wars.

Some of these defeated nations included those residing in or near the present-day boundaries of Pennsylvania:
> * The Eries (northeast Pennsylvania)
> * The Neutrals (to the west of the Iroquois & north of Lake Erie)
> * The Susquehannocks (southern Pennsylvania and along both
> North and West Branches of the Susquehanna River)

By the middle of the 18th century, the Iroquois League could lay claim to the lands of interior Pennsylvania.

In these Beaver Wars, the League had also defeated such Algonquian [8] Native American nations as the Huron, whose homelands were to the north and west of the League. The famous French explorer, Samuel de Champlain, had helped the Hurons defeat the Iroquois in battle in the early 1600's. Hence the Iroquois became traditional enemies of the French because of: [9]
> * the French being allied with the Hurons
> * the fur trade

By utilizing this position of the "middleman", the League could trade with Indian nations to their north and west and sell the furs so obtained from these natives to the Dutch at Albany (New York), the Swedes along the southern Delaware (Pennsylvania and Delaware), and the English in Maryland. In turn, they could sell or barter European trade goods to the Native American nations to their north, west and south.

Throughout the last half of the 17th century, the League fought wars to secure and protect their trade, once established; and to secure their homeland borders. Flexing their emerging military power, in the 1680's, they lay seige to the French city of Montreal.

The League thus became very powerful and greatly respected by the growing European colonies of France and Great Britain. This occurred despite the fact that at their maximum power, they could field collectively perhaps 2200 warriors, out of a population estimated at 12,000. By the last half of the 17th century, their influence was felt as far west as the Illinois River; east to the Kennebec River (in Maine); south to the Tennessee River; and north to Ottawa. [10]

Over the centuries, the Iroquois, like other Eastern Woodlands Indians, had borrowed technology, rituals, decorative motifs, and many other cultural traits from their Native American neighbors. It is possible that this characteristic helped to form the League since after several generations, if not centuries, of borrowing from each other, even cultures dispersed across a large geographic area would begin to have common characteristics. Though the dialects of each nation differed, the five original nations had a common language grouping: Iroquoian. They developed *in situ*. They were clustered in one geographic area. It is possible that these also were reasons why the Confederacy could be formed.

A reason which certainly helped solidify the League dealt with politics and their government. The Council House at Onondaga, the League's capital, symbolically faced east and west, if not physically, and in and of itself symbolized the unity of the League: embracing the eastern Mohawk as well as the western Seneca and all nations between. [11] It was located in the territory of the Onondaga, along a main Iroquoian trail running from present-day Albany, NY to Niagara Falls. [12] At the time of the American Revolution, this trail was known as the Ambassador's Road. [13] The Onondaga Iroquois themselves were in a central location common to all League members. At Onondaga (near present-day Syracuse, New York) at least once a year the Great Council met. Much time was given for deliberation of an issue and each member nation delegation had time to present their case. [14] Ideally, no major action could be taken by the League until it spoke as one; thus unanimous consent was the goal of their problem-solving and decision-making process. [15]

The strategy of the Iroquois in international diplomacy was to play one nation against the other: the French and their Canadian territory against the British and their colonies. With an European ally, the Native American could bargain from a position of strength.

The League's strengths were its:
* unity
* geographic position in relationship to European/colonial civilizations and other Native American nations
* reputation as a military power.

The Confederacy's reputation was so established within Great Britain's northeastern colonies that Pennsylvania's Indian policy was first and foremost created to meet the needs of the Iroquois. Thus, if the Iroquois claimed to own Pennsylvania-coveted lands, the Penns and their agents believed them.

All major Indian land purchases within the colony of Pennsylvania after 1737 (the year of the Walking Purchase, involving the Delaware), were made with the Iroquois. At Shamokin, PA, sat the Cayuga sachem, Shikallemy, empowered with overseeing the Delaware. The Iroquois invited various Indian nations to settle on lands they, the Iroquois, owned (either hereditarily or by military conquest), in order to act as a buffer between encroaching white civilization and their native territory.

The Iroquois also attempted to establish a permanent land boundary between Indian lands, primarily their own and those they claimed they owned (including the Ohio Valley). In 1768, at the Treaty of Fort Stanwix, a boundary was established separating colonial lands and settlements from Indian. In terms of Pennsylvania, this boundary generally ran southwest from Tioga (Athens, PA) along Tiadachton Creek. There exists some discrepancy as to whether this was the present Pine Creek or Lycoming Creek. [16] From Tiadachton Creek, the boundary ran to the north bank of the West Branch of the Susquehanna, extended westward to the headwaters of the West Branch, further west to the Kiskiminetas River and the mouth of the Allegheny, westward still down the Allegheny to the confluence of the Ohio River, down the northwest bank of the Ohio to the beginning of the Virginia-Kentucky settlement. The southern terminus was the confluence of the Tennessee River with the Ohio River (Paducah, KY). [17] (See Figures 4.1 and 4.2.)

The former allies of the French, such as the Shawnee and Delaware, were not pleased that the Iroquois had sold their reestablished lands without their consent. Perhaps the Iroquois felt that if the whites wanted land, this agreement would ease the encroaching pressure upon them. Even the colonial and British governments were not expecting such liberal boundaries. Sir William Johnson, British Indian Superintendent, became a land speculator, buying large parcels of land.

It is interesting to note that the Treaty placed the "Keepers of the Eastern Door", the Mohawks, entirely within the white settlement boundaries. To a great extent, the Mohawks were forced to rely upon the British Government, represented by Sir William Johnson, to maintain their agreed-upon territories in land disputes involving New York settlers. [18]

Trade helped create the Confederacy's power. Trade and contact with European civilization helped destroy it and its culture. Archaeological investigations of Onondaga and Oneida villages suggest that European trade goods replaced almost all native crafts by the end of the 17th century. Iron and brass kettles replaced clay pots. Metal knives and axes replaced those of stone. [19] The gun replaced the bow and arrow. The Mohawks were one of the earliest nations to use guns, as they were supplied by the Dutch in Albany, NY. Noting the large numbers of clothing items listed in trade accounts from the 1690's, one researcher concluded that it was difficult to imagine the Iroquois in anything other than European clothing after this time. [20]

By the mid 1700's, the rate of change in the Iroquois culture escalated. An excavated long house (a typical physical dwelling housing single to numerous families within it) in Onondaga County, New York, prior to this time period had measurements of 334 feet in length by 23 feet in width. [21] At Onaquaga, a village along the Susquehanna River in Southern New York occupied by the Oneida and Tuscarora, a visitor in 1769 noted that the Iroquois lived in typical longhouses measuring approximately 50 to 100 feet long and 20 feet wide, with bark roofs, no chimneys, and no windows. Each home was home to about six families. [22] Just 10 years later (1779), the same town was described as having dwellings on each side of the river, consisting of well-

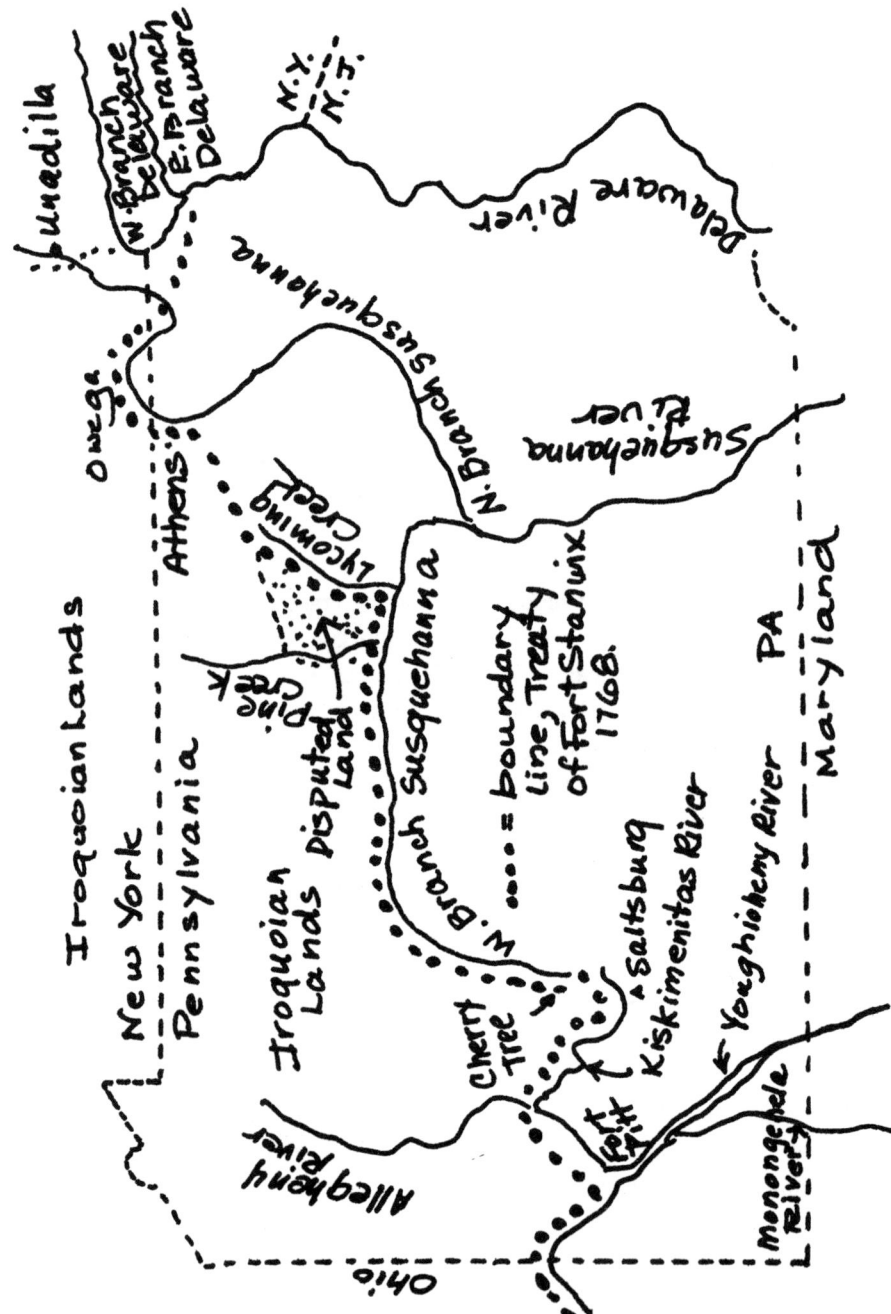

Figure 4.1. Boundary Line of the 1768 Treaty of Fort Stanwix, pertaining to present-day Pennsylvania and New York (not drawn to scale).

20

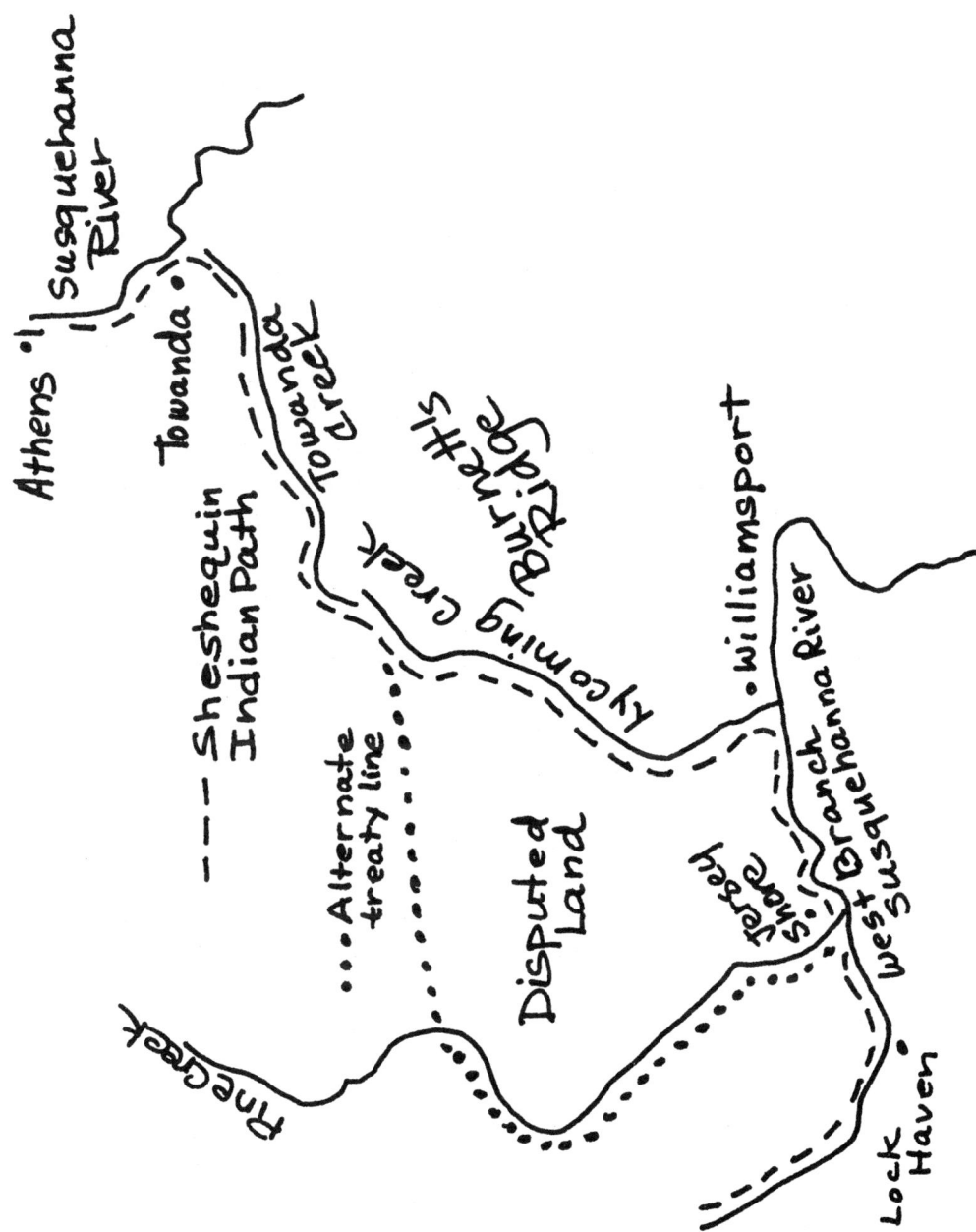

Figure 4.2. Treaty Line: Treaty of Fort Stanwix. The author believes that the correct path follows the Sheshequin Indian Path. (Not drawn to scale.)

constructed log houses with stone chimneys and glass windows. [23]

Changes to less tangible aspects of Iroquois culture were perhaps even more profound. The fur trade totally upset the Iroquois economic system. Time and energy were expended obtaining pelts, and basic subsistence activities like hunting, gathering, and farming, were neglected. Post-European contact Onondaga and Oneida villages were considerably smaller than earlier villages. [24] This fact suggests that the traditional economy based on hunting and agriculture could no longer support the same number of people. The role of women undoubtedly changed, since many of the things they produced, namely clay pots, baskets and clothing, had been replaced by trade goods. Even the sacred realm of Iroquois life was affected. Iroquois healers, individuals recognized as being in closest contact with the spirit world, were powerless against the European diseases. Despite their best efforts, people died. Did the Iroquois feel that the spirits had deserted or become angry with them?

Among the American Indians of the Eastern Woodlands, including the Iroquois, power was the key to life. It was widely distributed by gender and individuals with power could successfully interact with other people, grow crops, slay animals and defeat enemies. Men's power lay in the ability to control weapons and animals; women's power was related to the ability to bear children and grow crops. Rituals and ceremonies secured power for individuals and courted the favor of powerful spirits; power was lost and spirits were annoyed when rituals were neglected. [25]

This notion of power as the key to all life, and the need for rituals associated with it, were not understood by most European colonists. Europeans, of course, were no strangers to power, and many had travelled to this new world in search of power. For the colonists, power was gained through land ownership, the accumulation of wealth, political success, and religious freedom. Both Indian and colonist were at a disadvantage when it came to interpreting each other's actions -- they could only do so by looking through the filters of their own cultures. In spite of changes sweeping their culture, the Iroquois held on to many customs and traditions up to and through the American Revolution (1775-1783).

All of Iroquoian society was divided into clans named for certain revered animals. The clans permeated each original five nation member of the League. Marriage within one's clan was taboo. For example, a Mohawk Bear clan member might not marry a Bear clan from the Seneca, the Cayuga, or other member nations, for all these clan members were considered brothers and sisters. Thus one would be marrying one's relatives. Other clans included the Turtle, Wolf, Deer and Beaver. Such arrangements also included the Tuscarora, the step-brother nation, who had in common with the founding nations the Deer and Beaver clans. [26]

The league practiced matrilineal descent, giving women unique power. Each clan was entitled to a certain number of chiefs, political (sachems) and military. The clan mothers (matrons) of these clans could appoint and depose these chiefs. Thus, if a chief died, his title did not automatically pass on to his son. Titles were hereditary only within the clan. The son belonged to his mother's clan, not that of his father. Thus the title would be inherited by one of his brothers (if he had one), or one of his sister's sons, or another male member in his clan matron's lineage. [27]

Iroquois women exercised their power in numerous ways. Women, through choosing the sachem, could always make their wishes and those of "the people" known in council. When the council was deadlocked, they referred the issue to a council of clan mothers. [28] They also could make or break a war party by either supporting or disapproving the warrior's mission using such tactics as withholding supplies of moccasins and charred corn (cornmeal sweetened with maple sugar). These duties were carried out by the women as the "voice of the people." [29]

However, this held only for the "aristocratic women" - those carrying the aforementioned authority. Those from the wrong families, those in nonnoble positions of authority, had no power; and their offspring inherited the wind. [30]

The Iroquois Confederacy had only two hereditary war chiefs. These belonged to the Seneca, specifically within the Wolf Clan and Turtle Clan. Being the Guardians of the Western Door, the Seneca were the first line of defense against danger on the frontier. Thus was the reasoning handed down from time in memoriam, in the eternal legends involving the creation of the League. The Seneca were also the most populous of the League and the least dependent on the British. During the Revolution, these two heriditary chiefs were Cornplanter and the much elder statesman, Sayenqueragtha, who did not like Joseph Brant. [31] Sayenqueragtha, whose white name was "Old Smoke", belonged to the Turtle Clan; Cornplanter to the Wolf Clan. Sayengaragtha stood over six feet tall, and was a noted, powerful orator. At the time when the Iroquois took up the hatchet with the British, he was 70 years old [32] and was influential within his nation.

During the French and Indian War, some Seneca principally sided with the French, abandoning the 1701 Covenant with the English and French in which the Iroquois pledged neutrality to both sides. During Pontiac's Conspiracy, some fought against the English. Mohawks, under Sir William Johnson, Superintendent of Indian Affairs, opposed them. A young Mohawk warrior, Joseph Brant, fought alongside Johnson, but the Seneca had long memories. Brant had no influence with this nation when he attempted to rally them to the English side at the very beginning of the Revolution. [33]

Fighting actively for the British during the French and Indian War, the Mohawks could field approximately 250 warriors. This war cost them close to 100 warriors. This was a great loss, considering that at the beginning of the American Revolution, they had approximately 160 men in their entire nation. [34]

The two previous paragraphs refer to several important points:
(1) The British overestimated Joseph Brant's influence among the Iroquois. It was not until nearly the end of the Revolution, when Brant married his third wife, Catherine, who was within clan lineage (a matron) and the daughter of the Pennsylvania trader George Croghan, that he acquired influence among the Mohawks. It was Brant's sister, Molly, a clan matron and mistress of Sir William Johnson, who had influence.

(2) Brant was a brilliant Mohawk war chief who rose to prominence outside clan heredity (this could be done in Iroquoian society). But given the limited

numbers of his followers, he could not possibly have been everyplace as reported by the New York and Pennsylvania patriots during the Revolution. For example, they had connected him with and included him present at the infamous Wyoming Massacre. He wasn't there. [35]

(3) Brant's followers consisted not only of the remnants of the Mohawk nation but also of *loyalists*: whites siding with the British. They were named Brant's Volunteers - an official British military unit with the British Northern Indian Department. Many "Mohawks" were, in reality, whites dressed as Indians. [36]

The strategy of Iroquois diplomacy was to play off one nation against another, as previously stated. Tactics implement strategy. The reputation of the Iroquois rested upon their proven military prowess. Military tactics, in turn, rested upon hit-and-run raids which offered the least chance of loss of numbers. To be sure, Indians could and would offer head-on pitched batteries. Hence the Shawnee standing for hours line to line with the Virginia militia at Point Pleasant (located in what is now West Virginia) during Lord Dunmore's War in 1774. Hence the Iroquois offering battle to Sullivan at Newtown, NY, in 1779, even though they faced artillery and were outnumbered approximately 10-1.

It was in the frontier raid that the Indian gained his fearsome reputation. Approaching the targeted area, a raiding party would disperse into several smaller groups, often striking simultaneously.

Tactics existed within tactics: a surprise volley in ambush - using trade guns, rifles or smoothbores; the rush into the white opponent's ranks with the scalping knife, the war club, the spear and the tomahawk, before the surprised opponents could give any powerful volley of fire back. (The Mohawks were the first to acquaint themselves with firearms, supplied by the Dutch from Albany in the 17th century.) With "war paint", warriors made themselves hideous looking on purpose to frighten the enemy. Modern psychology recognizes that in extreme stress, past learning is forgotten. Training a man received (if any) in how to fire his gun or to get into and maintain formation literally could be frightened out of him.

Wounded prisoners would be killed and scalped on the spot, some being tortured first. Who knows what whims set off the Indian warrior when his adrenaline was "up"? There appeared to be rationality behind it. Perhaps it was known that wounded prisoners (those out of self-control), given their stress level and physical problems, could never make it back to their native villages, Niagara, or any other point. They would be easy to trail by the enemy, slowing down the war party in its escape. Reading accounts and records of both sides (patriot and British), it appears as if a "controlled assertive behavior stance", nonaggressive, nonassertive, given absence of major physical wounds, stood the best chance of survival. (See also Footnote 25.)

Woe to the person who tried to escape and failed. Warrior enmity knew no bounds in such situations.

On the humane side of the native nature of war, prisoners would be adopted into the Iroquoian village by the family of the slain warrior. In this way, lost manpower was replaced. However, one more obstacle remained for the patriot made prisoner: running the gauntlet. (See Section 11.) If he physically survived this ordeal, he could be assured of adoption or passed on to the British as a prisoner who might subsequently be exchanged.

Misunderstood by both sides - rebel and the King's cause - was the importance of culture in Indian military tactics. The Indian warrior must grieve the loss of his comrades-in-arms. Their limited numbers reinforced this practice. The surviving warriors were obliged to return home and grieve with the bereaved relatives. Whites, who saw Indians leaving after a battle, interpreted this behavior as capriciousness or cowardice. [37]

Scalps *were* taken. A symbol of a warrior's courage, an enemy's scalp was placed in a small hoop, dried and painted red around the edge, and was treasured by the warrior. A proof of courage, it made a gift to the family who had lost a loved one. Though such a family preferred a prisoner whom they could adopt to take the place of the departed warrior, they would take the hooped scalp in replacement if offered. It became a reminder of the deceased, particularly if he had been killed in battle. [38]

The Iroquois Council could come to unanimity on policy but the council had no coercive power over League members, only League "moral authority" and tradition. Hence it was the missionary to the Oneida Nation, Samuel Kirkland, who sided with the patriots, who held the Oneidas neutral when the Confederacy, after the Battle of Oriskany (see Footnote 42), decided to fight alongside the British. [39] Samuel Kirkland had been chaplain in the Sullivan Expedition.[40] Some Oneida warriors fought in General John Burgoyne's 1777 Expedition, siding with General Horatio Gates and the patriot forces opposing Burgoyne. [41]

Daniel Claus, former British Superintendent for Indian Affairs of Canada, the Northern District of the Indian Department (see below), and Assistant Superintendent of Indians on the St. Leger Expedition [42], claimed it was he who devised the stratagem to get the Iroquois to break their neutrality and side with the King. [43]

In a treaty signed at Albany, NY, during August of 1775, the League had pledged its neutrality to the rebelling colonies. [44] As the King's quarrel with his "sons" developed, the League had also pledged neutrality to the British.

The British Northern Department, through the Colonial Secretary's Office in London, determined policy for New York and Pennsylvania, the northern Great Lakes states, and Canada. This was overseen by the Governor of Canada. Within the Northern Department existed the Northern District of the Indian Department, headquartered at Fort Niagara (present-day Niagara Falls, NY). Prior to the Revolution, Sir William Johnson was Superintendent of Indian Affairs of the Northern District of the Indian Department. After his death, he was succeeded by Guy Johnson, Sir William's nephew and son-in-law. During the early years of the Revolution, the Governor of Canada was Sir Guy Carlton. [45]

The original policy of the British Colonial Office and the Northern Department, through the Governor of Canada and the Northern Department Superintendent of Indian Affairs, was to keep the Iroquois *neutral, but in a state of readiness* to fight on the side of the King. This policy was to be implemented by the Northern District of the Indian Department. [46]

By 1777, this policy had shifted. New instructions were received from the Colonial Secretary. The British, in the planned 1777 offensive led by General John Burgoyne and his army (invading south through Lake Champlain and the Hudson River Valley), were now to actively seek the support of the Iroquois [47]: their "state of readiness" was to be transformed into active war.

John Butler (see Section 5) was appointed in late 1775 by Governor Carlton as Guy Johnson's Deputy and accorded the rank of major in the Indian Department. [48] He had been sent to Fort Niagara to implement the first British Indian policy: neutrality but in readiness. Now he had new instructions, to the effect: "Instigate the Iroquois to join us," - i.e., the British.

Cajoled through councils, rum and presents, the Iroquois were "invited along" on the St. Leger expedition and urged to "come and watch us" defeat the rebels - "Bostonnais", as Brant referred to them. This was the stratagem that Claus claimed was his idea. For warriors to watch a battle and not participate is akin to a thirsty man in the desert refusing a drink of water. It is unclear from the records of the actual events what factor turned the Iroquois League into an active participant in the St. Leger campaign. Perhaps it was the Three Rivers council held 5 miles south of Oswego. [49] The final outcome was that the Iroquois fought with the British provincial forces (rangers in the Indian Department and Sir John Johnson's Royal Yorkers ["Johnson's Greens" under Sir John Johnson, white son of Sir William Johnson]). [50]

They, the Iroquois, helped lay siege to Fort Stanwix and fought in the Battle of Oriskany on August 6, 1777, against Herkimer (refer to footnote 42) and their brothers, the Oneida, who fought for Herkimer.

The Onondaga Long House was ripped asunder. The history of the League was forever changed.

Land was certainly an issue in this clash of civilizations. One culture, the native indigenous people, revered the land and its resources within a sense of community. European-based culture used the land and claimed it on an individual basis, with distinct boundaries. Once it was used up, he moved on.

There was a final and most important reason for the Iroquois to side, primarily, with the British: trade. In spite of a public image of assertiveness, the Iroquois were dependent upon European and/or colonial manufactured goods. Rebel or king, the side that would provide the best goods held the Indians as allies.

The Indian became dependent upon the trader for the rifle, lead, powder and flints to hunt upon the land; without these, he could not hunt. The old traditions were breaking away; he no longer used the bow and arrow. Blacksmiths were needed to repair the guns. Metal pots were superior to clay. Glass beads were important for wampum belts, which served as memory of treaties and the ever-increasing complexity of life. Paint was necessary for both ceremony and war.

Kelsay asks these questions: were the traditional ways of the Iroquois intrinsically better than the emerging new? Was their culture truly that of the "noble savage" in harmony with nature? Were they inferior to European civilization? or simply different? Regardless, as Kelsay reveals, there were facets to their culture that placed them in ever-increasing disadvantage with Euro-American civilization the more they were in contact with it. (And the greater the contact, the less stable was their environment.) Some of these characteristics and disadvantages listed by Kelsay are: [51]

> * *Gossip.*
> They were fond of gossip - both men and women. The Iroquois thus fell prey to those whites who would purposely tease them with rumors of some landowner purchasing his hunting territory. The Mohawk, enveloped within the boundary line established by the Fort Stanwix Treaty, 1768, were particularly susceptible to this.
>
> * *No written alphabet.*
> The Iroquois had wampum belts as mnemonic (memory cue) devices. He had no written alphabet. The wampum belts represented his oral traditions, the culture of his nation, treaties, etc. Now there were copious treaties - ever increasingly complex. Now there appeared strange small symbols which the whites said represented their permission to sell the land (legal certificates; deed

titles; surveyor's reports; legal ajudications; contracts; etc.).

* *Liquor.*
More than likely, the Native American did not invent fermented drink. The European introduced liquor to the Native American (not just the Iroquois), who rapidly took a liking to it; and it rapidly got him inebriated.

Plied with liquor, the Iroquois lost all restraint. This held true for both men and women. Inebriated, they would even fight each other.

Liquor thus led to both disintegration of the individual's life and societal chaos.

Plied with liquor, crops did not get planted.

* *Land concepts.*
Plied with liquor, and/or quantities of trade goods, an Iroquois or any other Native American, could affix his symbol to a piece of paper and sell the land out from under the entire village or tribe. [52] For the Native American in the Northeast US, there was no individual ownership of land. How could a person own the land? This was a foreign concept. Since the Indians had no concept of individual land ownership, they had no idea of what this concept of land ownership would mean to them.

For this individual, he probably felt that the whites were foolish enough to offer him liquor and trade goods for something he did not own to begin with. Well, he would take it.

For the Euro-American, practicality entered into this picture. Time is short. The best bottom land will be gone. It was far quicker and cheaper to deal with one or two Indians than wait months for a whole nation, or even a village, to assemble in council, feeding and providing for them while they deliberated. Meantime, all this land - its just *empty.*

Even the European nations such as France and Great Britain, regarded the Native Americans as *subjects* - not as sovereign nations, even though they negotiated treaties with them. "Subjects" implies already owning the land. This, of course, was never officially stated to the Native American.

* *Numbers.*

The Iroquoian culture did not emphasize precise number systems, as did Europeans. They were not "on time" for starts of treaty deliberations with the Europeans, who thrived on chronological time, precise mathematical calculations in surveys, boundary markers, etc.

An example: "to the setting sun" might mean to the top of the next ridge where one can see the sun setting. To the Euro-American, survey measurements of such a ridgeline might be interpreted to be the starting point from which to advance as far west as possible.

* *Disease.*

The Native American had no acquired immunity over the eons to European diseases such as smallpox or tuberculosis. This decimated populations. Decimated populations result in loss of leadership, in loss of men trained in social functions such as healing; men trained since boyhood to remember the wampum belts and what they meant; men trained as warriors; etc. Who would teach the new captives adopted into the village the ways of our people? What were the ways?

* *Material goods.*

Recall, reader, the concept of power (footnote 25) and that power permeated all levels of life. Though attached to his traditional customs, the Iroquois could see that European trade goods created less work. The old ways were labor intensive. Everything from guns to saw blades. Even glass beads to replace the wampum shell beads. The more he acquired, the more he wanted.

Perhaps a young warrior thought, "Why risk life on a raid to the distant Illinois or to the Catabas (the Carolinas)? Why, just across the river or just over the ridge, stood cattle, horses of the English. They seem to have so much of what I want and need. And they are so many."

Thus, presents and plunder became objectives of the Native American's way of life, fired by liquor.

* *Warfare.*
Recall the concept of the "mourning war" (footnote 37), and how European trade goods escalated, intensified this cultural trait.

The Iroquois shared what he had with family, friends, and those in need. And there were always those in need. There were always hungry periods in any given year, even if the crops were planted. This state of need was not helped by being cheated by a trader in his bartering and/or sale of hides, pelts, and other natural products to the trader.

Having placed more and more reliance upon European material goods, having experienced the "good life" represented by these goods, warfare presented the opportunity to acquire these goods - either as presents or as plunder. Why keep "the old ways" with all the intensive labor required to produce "now-inferior" goods? Why develop for the future if goods and opportunity for plunder can be provided now?

To a needy people, dependent more and more upon liquor and European trade goods, having fewer people due to warfare and having less land upon which to farm and hunt due to land sales, which contributed to the greater dependence upon trade goods, the British storehouse seemed never empty.

The Iroquois thus sided with the British during the American Revolution for three major reasons:

(1) Oriskany and their culture. The concepts of power and the mourning war mixed with death in battle. The spirits of those slain had to be avenged.

(2) The British could supply them with goods. The supply and quality seemed never to end.

(3) It appeared, to the Iroquois, that it was the Colonials who were constantly encroaching upon and buying the land. At least the British, as represented by their Indian Superintendent, Sir William Johnson, would speak for them in legal issues. Was it not the British King who helped negotiate the final land boundary with these colonists (the Treaty of Fort Stanwix, 1768), forever establishing permanent lands for the People of the Long House?

British rangers.

Section 5:
Butler's Rangers: Winged Retribution
(Frankstown Combatants)

In the February of the Hunger Moon (see Section 1), 1780, rangers and Iroquois war parties were on the move. With Sullivan, the war on the New York and Pennsylvania frontiers moved into a new, uglier phase based on revenge and vigorous retaliation. [1] Toward the end of 1780, these results for the year were reported by Colonel John Butler, head of Butler's Rangers: [2]

- 59 war parties from Niagara between February 3rd and September, 1780, with 16 parties still out on the frontiers. The latter parties involved 892 men (including Indians); the former, 1403 men.
- Recorded rebel losses:
  - 142 killed
  - 161 taken
  - 81 women and children released
  - 247 horses and 922 cattle taken
  - 157 houses destroyed
  - 150 granaries destroyed

This did not account for strictly Indian raids, other provincial forces such as Brant's volunteers, Johnson's Greens, etc. Northumberland County, PA, settlements alone in that year experienced 17 raids with these results: [3]

- 15 militia killed, including 13 at the Battle of Sugar Loaf Mountain (near Hazleton, PA) involving 31 militia. Several militia were taken prisoner at this battle, including the commander, Lt. Myers.
- Shickshinny Mills burned after the Battle of Sugar Loaf Mountain
- 4 rangers killed in a skirmish, near present-day Mifflinburg
- 5 settlers shot
- 18 settlers killed
- 20 prisoners taken, 7 escaped

John Butler was commander of Butler's Rangers. He initially held the rank of major in the Indian Department, in 1776, when he was appointed deputy to Guy Johnson, Superintendent of Indian Affairs since the death of his father, Sir William, in 1774. Sir Guy Carlton, the Governor of Canada, had ordered Butler to Niagara with instructions to hold the Indians neutral until further orders. [4] Butler and 67 recruited loyalists joined the St. Leger expedition (see Section 4) in 1777. After the lifting of the Fort Stanwix siege by Benedict Arnold and St. Leger's return to Canada, Butler led his men back to Fort Niagara and by himself proceeded to Quebec. In the Chateau St. Louis in Quebec City, the official residence of the king's government of Canada, on September 15, 1777, Governor Carlton signed a "beating order" for Butler to raise a corps of rangers. [5] When the corps was two-thirds full, Butler was to be commissioned a lieutenant colonel of provincials.

John Butler, born in 1725, was a farmer, experienced woodsman, French and Indian War veteran [6] and had served as an interpreter in the Indian Department under Sir William Johnson's direction. His father, Walter, had been a close friend of Sir William and had acquired 60,000 acres on the north side of the Mohawk which he named Butlersburg. Walter Butler had been a British officer for 70 years. Upon his death in 1760, John inherited the estate. His house, inherited from his father and built in 1742, still stands in Fonda, NY. [7] One of John's sons, Walter, became a captain in the ranger corps and served as second in command from the fall of 1778 until his death in October, 1781. [8]

John Butler, 52 years of age when commissioned a major in the rangers, has been described as physically stocky and short, with a snub nose, and possessing intense, staring eyes. [9] Psychologically, he allegedly possessed the characteristic of often repeating himself when excited. Governor General Frederick Haldimand, Carlton's successor as governor, described the father as lacking in education and the son as conceited. [10] Upon the conclusion of the Wyoming campaign, Butler gave up field command and returned to Fort Niagara in poor health, suffering from "the ague" [11] (malaria) [12]. Seldom again would Butler take the field in personal command. Was his health the excuse? Rumors in Fort Niagara were that he was tired of Indian affairs and wished he could be through with them. [13]

The Butlers were not the only father-son team in the rangers. Another ranger officer destined to play a role at Frankstown was Lieutenant Robert Nelles. His father, Hendrick William Nelles, also had land north of the Mohawk and lived not far from John Butler. He, too, was a veteran (lieutenant) of the French and Indian War. Early in the Revolution, he felt so strongly for the king's cause that he abandoned his wife and eight sons to serve and joined the Indian Department under Guy Johnson. His wife and children were subsequently rescued from rebel territory in eastern New York by the British army commander at Fort Niagara, Lieutenant Colonel Mason Bolton. Robert, his eldest son, also rescued at this time, enlisted in the Indian Department and was commissioned lieutenant. Both Hendrick and Robert Nelles survived the Revolution. [14]

In Section 4, the reader saw that British strategy was originally to keep the Iroquois neutral and then, by 1777, to induce them to join their side as participants in the ill-fated Burgoyne and St. Leger campaigns. Great Britain did not have the numbers of regular troops to fight a far-flung rebellion an ocean away. Therefore, she went shopping for troops in Europe, Canada and America. [15]

The British strategy for winning the war, as coordinated by the Colonial Secretary in London, involved the frontiers. Provincial troops and Indian allies were to:
* Destroy the granaries supplying rebel armies
* Divert troops from Washington's army for frontier defense
* Provision British provincial forces with captured supplies: cattle, horses, etc. (Recall from Section 1 that Niagara was logistically closed off from supplies for six months of the year.)

Troops were needed to implement strategy. Great Britain depended upon provincial forces from Canada, Indian allies, and loyalists from within the thirteen colonies. Canada, by the time of the Revolution, contained only 100,000 population; the thirteen colonies, approximately 2.5 million. [16] Sectors of strong Loyalist support (siding with the king's cause, also called Tory) in the colonies included Tryon County, NY; New York City; Philadelphia, PA; Southeast PA; North and South Carolina; Georgia; and strong pockets in New Jersey, Delaware, and Maryland. [17]

Within Pennsylvania, strong pockets of Loyalist support also existed in at least three of her frontier counties (Westmoreland, Bedford and Northumberland) and within the Wyoming Valley. [18] The latter was claimed by Connecticut which created the political jurisdiction, Westmoreland County (Connecticut). [19] One of the motives for rangers accompanying Butler's expedition against the Wyoming settlements was revenge. Many of the rangers on this expedition (along with 464 Indians - mostly Seneca and Cayuga) [20] were Pennsylvanians from the Wyoming Valley who had been dislodged, burnt from their homes by Connecticut settlers in the Yankee-Pennanite War between the colonies of Pennsylvania and Connecticut over claims to the Wyoming Valley. [21]

Besides revenge against Connecticut, there were other reasons why Pennsylvanians and New Yorkers were or became Loyalists or Tories: [22]
* Economics. The sale of grain for export to Europe was a major means of making a living. The export market was extinct, with ever increasing inflation. The upbeat of this was to blame it on the rebels (Whigs) for worsening their economic status.
* In Pennsylvania, on February 11, 1777, the government passed its first "Test Act". Every male over 18 had to take an oath of allegiance to the state or be disarmed and deprived of liberties, including the sale of land.
* Persons neutral, adhering to neither side (some estimates put the entire 13 colonies as much as 33% neutral, including slaves) [23] were suspected of siding with the enemy by local committees of safety. Such alleged collusion lead to confiscation of property, and/or jail for an individual and his family.
* Individuals (merchants, commercial interests, clergy, government officials, frontier settlers, etc.) who truly believed that their rights as Englishmen would be taken away by the rebels; that the king's cause was just.

During the entire war, from the year 1778 (when the corps of rangers was functional and implementing strategy), Butler's Rangers devastated

Pennsylvania's frontiers. Among the *principal* raids are these:
* Wyoming Valley, July 1-3, 1778, including: [24]
    * destruction of 1000 dwellings
    * destruction of all mills
    * loss of 1000 head of cattle, hogs, and sheep
    * destruction, capitulation of 8 forts
    * 140 prisoners
    * 446 lives lost (including defeat of the patriot forces July 3rd)
    * Abandonment of the West Branch of the Susquehanna River Valley with loss of 7 of its forts from Fort Reid (Lock Haven) to Fort Muncy (above Muncy, PA), driving the Northumberland County settlements back to Fort Augusta (Sunbury). [25]
* The capitulation at Fort Freeland, July 27, 1779, and the attempted ranger/militia rescue under Captain Hawkins Boone, a cousin of Daniel Boone. This rescue effort involved at least 22 casualties out of 36 or 37 men comprising the rescue force. The attack on the fort also lead to the killing of 5 defenders. In all, including male prisoners (the women and children were allowed to leave by the British and Iroquois for Sunbury and Fort Augusta), total casualties were 108. [26]
* Defeat of Phillips' Rangers near Saxton, PA, July 16, 1780. [27]
* Sugar Loaf Mountain, September, 1780 (near Hazleton, PA). (See above listing for Northumberland County.) [28]
* Frankstown, June 3, 1781
* Bald Eagle Creek, April 16, 1782
* Hannastown, July 13, 1782, in which the town was destroyed (the site of present-day Hannastown, PA) [29]
* Extermination of Colonel Archibald Lochry's expedition, in support of George Rogers Clark, August 24, 1782, eleven miles below the mouth of the Great Miami River, west of Cincinnati, Ohio. Lochry was County Lieutenant of Westmoreland County, PA. With him were 150 capable frontiersmen, including Captain William Stokeley's Rangers of Westmoreland County. Lochry and 36 others were killed; the rest were taken prisoners. Joseph Brant, the Mo-

hawk War Chief, lead the Indians and British in this ambush. [30]

By December, 1780, Butler's corps was full strength: 8 companies. Given his successes in Pennsylvania, New York, etc., in January 1781, Governor Haldimand gave now Colonel Butler permission to raise an additional two companies. At full strength in 1782, the ranger corps numbered 590 officers and privates. [31]

The first recruits were already veterans of the St. Leger expedition and the ill-fated rebel attempt to invade Canada in 1775. The first eight companies were organized in the fall of 1777. Two of these companies were to contain men who knew at least one Indian language, their customs and their methods of making war. The ranks in the other six consisted of men familiar with the forests and physically fit: able to endure fatigue. [32]

At full strength, a company was to number 58 men. Organized, each company had this structure and chain of command: [33]
- * Captain (one)
- * Lieutenant (one First or Second)
- * Sergeants (three)
- * Corporals (three)
- * Privates (fifty)

Enlistments, such as in all British provisional corps, would be for two years or until completion of the war. [34]

Pay scales, payable through the Indian Department in New York currency rates (see below), were as follows: [36]
- * Major-Commandant (position filled by Major, then Colonel Butler): 15 s. per diem (s. = shilling)
- * Captain: 10 s./diem
- * First Lieutenant: 3 s. 8 d./diem (d = pence)
- * Second Lieutenant: 3 s.. 8 d./diem
- * Corps Quartermaster: 4 s 8 d./diem
- * Corps Surgeon: 4 s./diem

Pay scales for those in other positions, payable through the Indian Department

in New York currency rates (see below) were as follows: [36]
* Sergeant: 5 s./diem
* Corporal: 4 s. 6 d./diem
* Drummer or private knowledgeable of Indian customs and able to speak an Indian language: 4 s. 6 d./diem
* Private: 2 s./diem

Sterling had the highest value of currency as compared with New York colonial currency circulating at the time. For example, a £5 note (5 pounds) in New York currency was really worth £2.18 s. 3 3/4 d. sterling. In sterling currency, a £5 note was worth £5. [37]

It can be seen that commissioned officers were paid more than non-commissioned ones and that men familiar with Indians and their languages received more pay.

Each man was to arm and clothe himself at his own expense. In the beginning, anything went in terms of uniform. Generally, they wore the typical hunting frock found on the frontiers: fringed, unpocketed, knee length, wrap-around secured with a belt. These, for a ranger, would be made of green linen. [38] Their legs would be protected by the 3/4-length Indian leggings made of animal hide and reaching to mid-thigh and secured by leather thongs to an inner belt, worn underneath the hunting frock. (See Figure 7.1.) On their feet would be moccasins, again made of hides. A typical moccasin would also have leather flaps which could be raised and wrapped around the ankle and lower shin and calf - held in place by leather thongs. [39] Headgear for Butler's Rangers consisted of either a leather or felt forage cap; if felt, it would be a cut down bicorne or tricorne hat. To these would be pinned cartridge case badges or brass belt plates for the purposes of identification. If leather, they would be engraved with the words "Butler's Rangers." [40]

Parade dress consisted of small coats (coates) made with dark green cloth, faced with dark red. The officers' uniforms were of better quality cloth. Pewter buttons for those in the ranks had stamped on them "Butler's Rangers". [41]

If not wearing Indian leggings, the uniform consisted of green or white coats and/or officer waistcoats. Overalls were of white linen. If the men wore breeches, they were made of wool or linen. The author cannot ascertain whether these whites were worn in the field or were solely for parade dress. Nor can he ascertain whether black buckled shoes were worn on expeditions. Perhaps buckled shoes made more sense than the moccasin in terms of Pennsylvania's rocky terrain. Rangers were indeed issued such shoes. [42] If moccasins were worn on expeditions, a necessity for supplies were a punch awl and needles, because moccasins had to be in constant repair. This held true for the Indian as well. To repair moccasins, hides would also be needed.

Rangers were strongly encouraged by Butler to have the rifled flintlock rather than the smoothbore musket, though some did have the latter. [43] The rifled flintlock had greater accuracy than the smoothbore; a ball could travel greater distance with more accuracy shot through a rifled gun: approximately 100-150 yards compared to 50 or 60 for the smoothbore. This advantage compensated for the smoothbore musket being able to be loaded quicker: 15 seconds compared to 30 for the "long rifle." [44] A man familiar with his own gun further helped marksmanship. Hence another reason why Butler probably encouraged men to bring their own rather than be given army issue. If Butler followed Rogers' Rangers tactics (which he generally did - see below) in terms of rifles, the length of the rifle barrel would be shortened to match the needs of bush fighting and browned to reduce the glare [45] as well as curtail a signal: the glint of the sun on a rifle barrel in a sea of green foliage is a dead giveaway - literally. Tomahawks and scalping knives would be other needed weapons of war.

Butler's Rangers, in terms of their operations throughout the war, can be divided into four phases: [46]
> (1) 1778-1779: raids upon the settlements, including those occupied by New Englanders. New England was a hotbed of Patriot sentiment; this was where the war started. Recall from above that Pennsylvania's Wyoming Valley was Connecticut's Westmoreland County.
> (2) Fighting Sullivan's army: 1779
> (3) Post-Sullivan: 1780-1781 raids that would retaliate for Sullivan's

expeditions.
(4) Post-Yorktown: 1781-1783 protection of the western Indian tribes allied to the British such as the Shawnees, Delawares, Wyandots (a branch of the old Huron nation) and Mingos. [47]

Permeating these phases were the goals of British strategy as listed above. Butler's Rangers and the Indian allies were the means, the tools, to implement British strategy. Tools of warfare, the rangers had set tactics used in any of these phases. These tactics principally followed the tactics developed by Roger's Rangers in the last French and Indian War, 1775-1763. John Butler himself was a veteran of this war. Tactics were devised for the terrain and the frontiers. The lessons inherent in Braddock's defeat in 1775 along the Monongahela River were needed. "On a scout," these included: [48]

* Never ford a river at a ford. The enemy expects it.
* If by boat, travel at night.
* Make camp *after* dark, never before, and always post your sentries in a spot with a clear view. Send out *teams* of sentries, six to a team and at least two on duty at a time.
* In force, march single file and space out; never leave a cluster of men for an enemy marksman. (Why? Such a cluster becomes the proverbial "broad side of a barn".)
* In large force, march in three columns, single file, the outer two at least 20 yards from the middle, and flanks forward, rearward and on all flanks. This makes it difficult to surround.
* If pursued, circle back and ambush the pursuer.
* If afoot in a swamp, march abreast to confound trackers.
* If engaged, *always*, but *always, avoid* firing in unison. Fire in teams. This always gives you firepower. This holds true in rushing the enemy: the front "line" (tree to tree) fires, drops and reloads while the next line advances through them. The same would hold true in retreat.
* On the march, keep a safe distance between you and any major stream. Why? The enemy has you between the water and them; the enemy's volley will "blow" you naturally away from the volley into open water. You will, in panic, move away from the danger. If still alive or unwounded, you become an *open* target and are further

hampered in mobility by water. Also, wet powder doesn't ignite.
(See footnote 44.) This last had implications at Frankstown.
Enduring fatigue, the ranger traveled light and covered great distances. The Indians, including Joseph Brant, taught the ranger: [49]
- * how to construct and use snow shoes.
- * how to make camp, how to make fire, and how to cook snow: all this in half an hour.
- * how to kill a rattlesnake and use it as rattlesnake soup as a cure for "swamp fever" or the "ague" (malaria).
- * how to use wild Solomon's Seal and broad leaf plantain as antidotes to rattlesnake bite.

The uncleared land of Pennsylvania and New York contained numerous swamps and bogs (the wetlands of today). In addition to hunger, fatigue, inclement weather and poisonous snakes, malaria was endemic. Mosquitoes ("muscetoes") were huge and swarmed in clouds. Is it any wonder that the Indian smelled because he used bear grease to keep insects away?

This, then, was the nature of frontier warfare. Add to this, reader, the need for constant attention while scouting to prevent ambush. Add to this the need to treaat wounds due to warfare in the middle of the forest. Add to this the fear of becoming separated from your guides or party and lost, even if you survived an ambush. Add to this the fear of torture if captured.

Furthermore, even Indians could get lost. Forest fires, wind and ice storms obliterate trails and landmarks - natural and man-made. Add to this the higher risk and incidence of infection of wounds due to this environment. Add to this the stench of a decaying body in the humidity of July and August as you attempt to bury "it" enough to keep it from being dug up by wolves and to lessen the risk of disease to you.

Add to this the weight of equipment and supplies. Add to this the need to build bark canoes or rafts to pole yourselves downstream [50] if the streams were high enough to propel you over the rocks. Add to this the need to continually repair your clothing and moccasins, torn and soaked from the swamps and bogs, and the need to keep your ramrod from breaking, your powder dry, and your gun as clean as possible so it would fire. These exclude your normal daily needs of excrement, hunger and thirst.

What thoughts exist about your family? Are they safe today? These thoughts may be saved for nighttime, as you place your bare, wet feet and moccasins toward the fire to dry in order to avoid the "scald feet": inflammation caused by continued friction between wet leather and wet skin (blistering). [51]

Nature knows no boundaries. She cannot be fenced in, like farmer's fields. The nature of this warfare existed the same for either side: the loyalist ranger as well as the patriot ranger; the loyalist Indian as well as those Oneida, Iroquois and Delaware fighting alongside the rebel militia and/or the rebel ranger.

Understand the above, reader, and you transcend time and space. Understand this, reader: Values held by men on either side or culture were so strong that they volunteered to undergo these hardships.

Forest warfare forced a change in tactics. Sullivan's and Brodhead's 1779 campaigns and Butler's own successes also forced modifications in tactics. The size of the raiding party was reduced. With the Indian's granaries, food storage, and villages destroyed and being driven closer to Niagara; with the successes of Butler driving in the frontiers of New York and in Pennsylvania (such as Northumberland County), the ranger and Indian ally naturally had longer distances to travel: both to reach the frontier and to return. After Sullivan, cattle would be used at times as pack animals, driven on raids to the settlements. Sacks of flour would be suspended over the cow's back to one side; salt to the other. From the records, the use of horses seems now to be more prevalent. The ranger now used horses sometimes rather than travelling on foot. Perhaps the horse would also help "herd" the carttle.

The nature of this type of warfare is indicative in Colonel Mason Bolton's (commander of the western posts, headquarters Fort Niagara) monthly report of the rangers dated October 6, 1780. Of 381 privates on the roster: [53]
    * 54 were present and fit for duty
    * 2 were recruiting

* 17 were rebel prisoners
* 1 was a new recruit
* 202 were in the field, from the Mohawk River Valley, NY, north to Canada, and west to Detroit. Of these, 4 were somewhere else in Indian country.
* 3 were on furlough
* 102 were sick in quarters.

Pennsylvania militia.

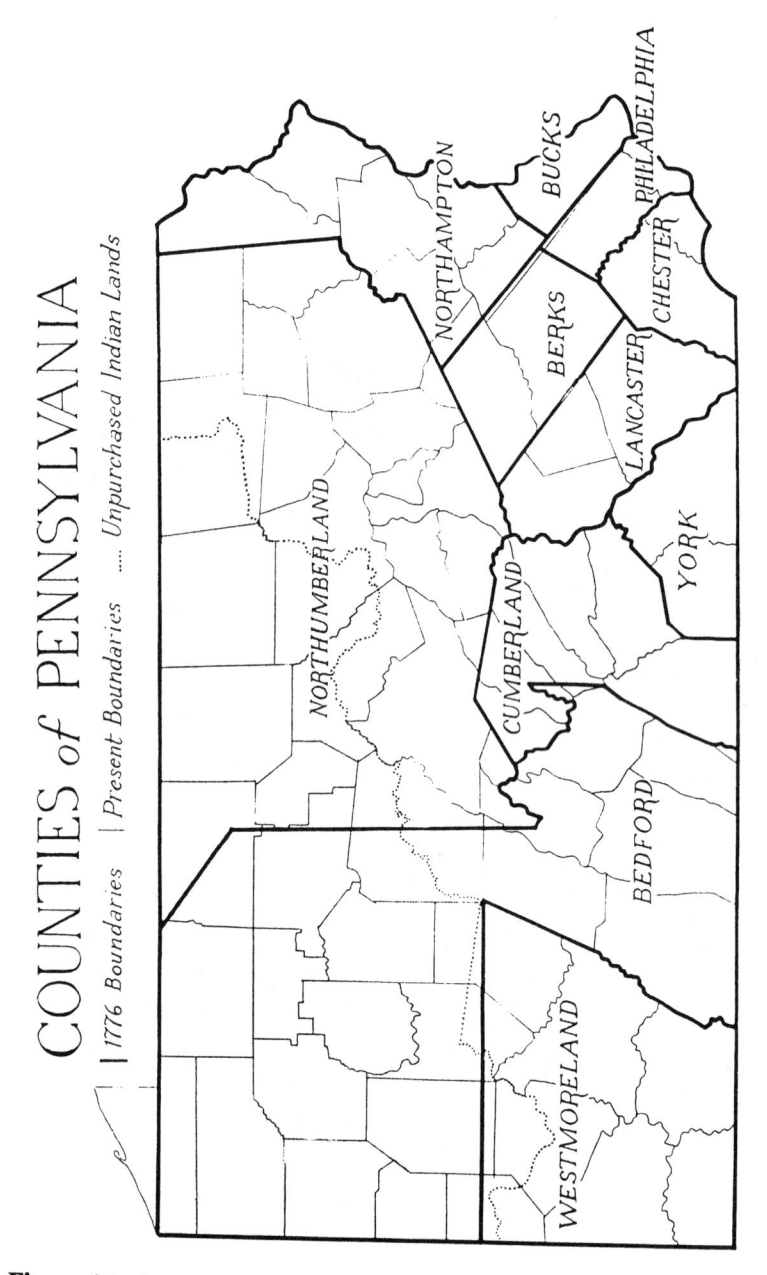

Figure 6.1. Counties of Pennsylvania. Map taken from *The Pennsylvania Line* by John B.B. Trussell. A publication of the Pennsylvania Historical and Museum Commission.

Section 6:
Pennsylvania Militia:
the Sword or the Plow?
(Frankstown Combatants)

The image of militia is well ensconsed in national folklore. The heroes of Lexington and Concord. The Minuteman. The intrepid march against all odds of George Rogers Clark through winter's swamps to take Vincennes and permanently claim the Illinois country for the rebel cause. Militia flocking to the Northern Continental army under General Philip Schuyler to stop the seemingly invincible Burgoyne. General Nicholas Herkimer, commander of the Tryon County, New York, militia at Oriskany, calmly directing the remains of the men while seated on a saddle propped up against a treee - while severely wounded in the leg.

Pennsylvania, too, had her militia. But by 1775, in the beginning of the war, Pennsylvania differed from the other colonies by being void of government sponsored military organization. This was due to the Quaker influence originating from the Quaker founder, William Penn. While the fighting continued in New England and moved to New York, Pennsylvanians voluntarily associated into armed companies. Hence the term *Associators*. In theory, men refusing to voluntarily enlist were termed Non-Associators. Suspected of loyalist sympathies, they would be disarmed, fined or punished. Men enrolled in such companies to avoid this, contributing to half-hearted support and morale problems. [1]

On March 17, 1777, the Pennsylvania legislature passed its first militia act. [2] This provided for compulsory service and covered white able-bodied men between the ages of 18 and 53. There were exceptions allowed: judges, ministers, legislators, members of the Supreme Executive Council (see below), faculties of colleges, servants and slaves. By the time the second act was passed in 1780, the number of exemptions was increasing. [3] It is interesting to note that members of the clergy were exempted but the male lay persons of the Quaker and Mennonite religious sects were not. These did not serve - act or no act.

The act called for the militia to be organized on a county-wide basis. For its defense, each county was placed under the supervision of a position called a *county lieutenant,* aided by sublieutenants. This was the equivalent of Great Britain's English lords lieutenant. [4] The county lieutenant in turn was answerable in the chain of command to the President of the Supreme Executive Council. The latter body itself had its origins in the Committee of Safety, organized by the legislature in 1775 and responsible for Colonial Pennsylvania's military forces. [5] (A map of counties formed by 1776 is found in Figure 6.1.)

The county lieutenant empowered a local official, such as a constable, to keep a roster of the male population. Given such a roster, the lieutenant and his subordinates would divide the county into militia districts. Each district would contain from 440 to 680 white men eligible for service. [6] A district was another name for a *battalion.* The districts themselves were political subdivisions of the county: several townships. Each district (or battalion) in turn was divided into eight *classes* (or companies), assigned a number *one* through *eight.* Class assignment was by lot. [7]

When needed for actual service, the militia was called out through this "class system": the first class first, the eighth class last, back to the first, etc. Each county was to furnish any given share of men in proportion to any other county. Furthermore, each county's militia were to serve the same period of time as any other county. [8] The goal of this system was equal representation of a county's commitment to frontier defense.

Battalion officers, colonels, lieutenant colonels, and majors were *elected* by the eight classes' (company's) officers comprising the battalion: captains, lieutenants and ensigns. These company officers were elected by those in their district who were eligible to vote for their General Assembly representatives. The county-wide officers were required to be resident freeholders within their district (on the tax roles). [9] This alone prevented some of the best officer potential in the state from serving. Within three months, the act was amended to read that such an officer could be any freeman. [10] The 1780 militia act ruled out the requirement of voting for colonel. [11]

Thus an inherent flaw was incorporated into Pennsylvania's militia command: Men could vote for someone they liked, who made tours of duty easy, rather than vote for them because of their expertise. Two other major flaws were:
* The act stipulated that tours of duty were for 60 days only.[13]
* The call had to emanate from the President of the Supreme Executive Council. [14]

The act also allowed for substitutes; failing this, a man might avoid service by paying a sum of money or a fine. By 1780, this sum was based on the value of a day's labor for each day he or any substitute was absent. [15]

Pennsylvania, at the time of the revolution, had three bonafide frontier counties: (See Figure 6.1.)
* Northumberland
* Bedford
* Westmoreland

Cumberland had been a frontier county devastated by Indian raids in the French and Indian War and Pontiac's Conspiracy (1763). She was now in transition, becoming more settled. Bedford was the frontier county protecting her western and northwestern flanks.

Bedford County's militia organization had the above structure. Colonel John Piper was, at the beginning of the war, the county lieutenant. However, Bedford County experienced several problems in its military organization in addition to the state wide flaws noted above. These particular problems were: [16]
* Indian raids commencing in 1777 drove much of the populton to the east and the south. The militia hence suffered from lack of manpower from which to draw their recruits.
* Early in the war, Bedford County sent militia companies east to fight with Washington's Continental Army. When their enlistments were over, the main army confiscated the men's personal arms (such

as flintlock rifles) originally brought with them.
* Political: Bedford County populace opposed Pennsylvania's ruling radicals. In retaliation, the state government appointed officials to county political office not having the confidence of the people. [17]

Two Bedford County officials, Thomas Smith and George Woods, described the above situations to President Reed of the Supreme Executive Council on November 27, 1777: [18]

> "...We keep out ranging parties, in which we go out by turns; but all that we do that way is but weak and ineffectual...because one half of the People are fled, those that remain are too busily employed in putting their families and what little of their effects that they can save and take into some places of safety, so that the whole burden falls upon a few of the Frontier Inhabitants. For those who are at a distance from danger have not as yet offered us any assistances, we are far from blaming the officers of the militia because they have not ordered them out, for if they had they really can be of little or no service, not only for the foregoing reasons, but also for these, not one man in ten of them is armed, if they were armed you are sensible and take the country through there is not one Fourth man that is fit to go against Indians, and it might often happen that in a whole class there might not be a single person who is acquainted with the Indian ways or the woods, and if there should be a few good Men and the rest unfit for service, those who are fit to take the Indians in their own way could not act with the same resolution and spirit as if they were sure of being properly supported by men like themselves. The Consequence would be that the Indians, after gaining an advantage over them, would become more daring and fearless and drive all before them. A small number of select Men would be of more real services the frontiers than six times that number of People unused to arms or the woods........"

The reader will note in the above another general problem with the militia in terms of frontier defense: unfamiliarity with the Indian tactics and their modes of warfare. This held particularly true for those interior, settled counties (for the frontier settler, the interior counties were those closer to the Atlantic seacoast) who would be ordered to send militia to the frontier county's aid. Such was the case with Cumberland County. When General Daniel Roberdeau first assembled the expedition for the building of Fort Roberdeau, in the spring of 1778, he requested aid of the Cumberland County militia from its county lieutenant, John Carothers. [19]

During the spring of 1778, Bedford County was rife with rumors, substantiated, that loyalists were about to descend on them. Approximately 30 Bedford County loyalists met near the lead mines (Sinking Valley, Blair County) started by General Roberdeau. They intended to rendezvous with Indians near Kittanning [20] and then raid Bedford County. Unfortunately for the loyalists but reversed fortune for the patriots, the Indians at Kittanning thought that these were rebel militia and fired on them, killing a loyalist leader, John Weston. The others escaped and fled back to Bedford County. John's brother, Richard, was captured and turned over to Roberdeau, who sent for Cumberland County militia to escort him to jail in Carlisle. During this time, fearing a major raid, Carothers ordered the Seventh and Eighth classes, Fifth Battalion, Cumberland County to Sinking Valley, Bald Eagle Valley, and Penns Valley (the latter two areas were political jurisdictions of Northumberland County, itself in dire straits at this time). Some of the militia sent to these last two places were not armed. [21]

Cumberland County militia remained in the above areas of Bedford County in May and June, 1778. During that summer, additional units were ordered to Standing Stone (now Huntingdon, PA) and the Kishocoquillas Valley (Lewistown, PA). Robert Cluggage, commander of Fort Roberdeau, reported that only 60 men arrived. [22]

In the spring of 1779, the Supreme Executive Council ordered 250 militia to both Bedford and Westmoreland counties in order to protect the settlers when they planted their spring crops. Again, turnout was less than anticipated. [23] One unit of Cumberland County militia ordered to Fort Roberdeau refused to go. [24]

Joseph Reed, President of the Supreme Executive Council, commenting on such events, stated: [25]

> "We ordered out 250 militia last April to march immediately to Bedford and Westmoreland, but even this, either from Real Inability, which can hardly be supposed, or from Real Aversion to the Service, has only been in part complied with. It is mortifying in two Respects, first, As it shews a Want of Attention to our suffering Friends on the Frontiers, and Secondly, as it discovers a Weakness in the Government."

Besides Reed, Smith and Woods, Northumberland County Lieutenant, Colonel Sam Hunter, from headquarters at Fort Augusta, was writing: [26]

> "I have Given orders for all that is Provided with arms to hold themselves in Rediness Imadiatly for their owen Defence. Yet there is a Great backwardness prevails with a number of the militia of this County in Regard of their situations, being with great propriety frontiers themselves, so that this is hard to turn out from their familys.
>
> "We are Badly off for Provisions, and Especially meat, as there is no Commissary appointed for thei County to Buy up such stores. And arms is very much wanted as there is not above seven Hundred and fifty that is fit for use, and sixty of the Publick arms, which is Very Ordinary. I give orders for a Company of Volintiers out of Each of the Batallions to be formed, which will do more service than all the militia of the County, for taking the People in Classes as their Tower [tour] of duty comes will not do to fight the Indians..."

Colonel Hunter raises a very pertinent point regarding the frontier settler: Would he serve a tour of duty in foreign lands while his own family might be in danger? Would a man serve to assist others to plant and harvest their crops when his *own* needed planted or harvested?

From diverse memorials and petitions come answers - such as the following from Northumberland County: [27]

> "The melencolly event of the 31st of May upon Loyalsock Creek oblig'd us to leave our homes and livings and to Assemble together in large Bodys in order to Protect our wives and Infant children from being victims of Savage fury...we have since frequently applied to Lieutenant of the County for aid, who after using his best Endeavours has not been able to furnish us with more than Seventy-three Troops of the Militia of this County to cover a Frontier of at least Forty miles in length. This supply we apprehend to be of little use, especially as their times will be out in the midst of Harvest..."

Problems of Pennsylvania's militia system were apparent by spring, 1778. Earlier in the war, on November 20, 1777, the Continental Congress appointed a three man Commission to investigate both the progress and further needs of Virginia and Pennsylvania for frontier defense. [28] By March, 1778, the three commissioners appointed had toured the environs of western Pennsylvania and then northwestern Virginia. In March, 1778 (the report is undated), they issued their findings to General Edward Hand, then Commander of the Western District and headquartered at Fort Pitt. The findings of this report, alluding to the problems inherent in any state's militia system, were: [29]

> "...The militia act of Pennsylvania limits the Service of its Militia to two months, but we think it would be proper your requisitions for Virginia should be for three months...We wish if practicable that instead of militia called out in the ordinary way, who are with difficulty brought to consider themselves soldiers, & will frequently abandon the most important enterprise in the moment of execution when their terms of service are about expiring, that you engage an equal number of volunteers to Serve for a longer time than can be expected or required of militia. The latter mode of protecting the country would, we believe, not only be more effectual, but more economical. We are, Sir, Your Most obedt humble Servts,"
>   Sam Mathews
>   Geo. Clymer
>   Saml. McDowell

These problems would have important consequences to the outcome of the battle June 3, 1781, at Frankstown.

Section 7:
Pennsylvania Rangers:
Traces of Honor
(Frankstown Combatants)

Ranger companies raised by the state of Pennsylvania were not militia, though they performed similar duties. These were created as military units to address the problems inherent in the militia service of the state.

Given over two decades of research, the author defines a ranger company as:
> A special military unit authorized by the state, paid and provisioned for a designated tour of service in a frontier county of Pennsylvania. Such a company differed from the militia in that:
> * Its tour of service was longer
> * It was to specifically engage in counter insurgency attacks of British-Tory and Indian raids while gathering intelligence for commanders of established military units: Continental army and militia.

Such state government sponsorship began in 1779, was reauthorized in 1780, and lasted through the end of the war.

It is difficult to ascertain exactly how many men served in Pennsylvania in such units. The historian and serious student must be careful in his/her research to distinguish such units from militia units who "ranged" between forts "on a scout". Furthermore, during the entire war, a man may have served in the Continental Army, received a discharge, gone home and helped in frontier defense in the militia, and later enlisted in a ranger company.

The Pennsylvania Archives lists approximately 11,400 men serving in ranging operations between 1778-1783; it states that a majority of these appear more than once on the list due to being paid for different tours of duty. [1] In Northumberland County, for example, from the late 1779-1783, ranger companies became the primary means of frontier defense. The author has found total depreciation payrolls of Northumberland County militia to contain 126 men who served in Captain Thomas Robinson's Ranging Company, formed in 1779, who survived the war. Post-war depreciation pay was given to compensate for the veterans not paid during the war due to collapse of wartime currencies and other financial obligations. [2] Excluded from these roles were seventeen of Captain Thomas Kemplin's company, formed in the spring of 1779. Thus in two primary companies from one county, the estimated numbers are 143.

Ranger companies served in the frontier counties of Bedford, Northumberland and Westmoreland (western Pennsylvania), which existed at the beginning of the war. Later in the war, Washington County was created from Westmoreland and became another frontier country. The original formation plans called for 380 rangers to serve in the three initial frontier counties which existed in 1779. (See Figure 6.1., Section 6 for boundaries of Bedford, Northumberland and Westmoreland Counties.)

Compounding the problem of research into Pennsylvania ranging companies for this historian is that, in the case of Westmoreland County, Colonel Daniel Brodhead had rangers taken from his Continental Line regiment - the 8th Pennsylvania. Technically, these were different from the definition given above, yet with the same listed duties. Furthermore, at the Battle of Fort Freeland, Kemplin's company served under the temporary command of Hawkins Boone, militia commander. Thus these men have never received the recognition due them. Only a few primary sources, mostly eyewitnesses, even mention the term "rangers" in association with this battle. On the other hand, militia at the engagement at Frankstown served under the command of Captain John Boyd, commander of Boyd's Rangers of Bedford County. Consequently, in terms of casualties for that engagement, several men who were fighting are counted as rangers. (See Section 8.)

The following is an orientation to supply understanding of the above definition and to help distinguish this type of service from the militia. Such an understanding is necessary in order to analyze the events of Frankstown. The genesis for the creation of ranger companies lay not only in the problems associated with the militia service. Colonel Samuel Hunter, County Lieutenant, Northumberland County, had convinced the Supreme Executive Council of the concept of six-month men by the end of 1778. [3] He had, at his own discretion, ordered out select men as "volunteers" from the militia (Section 6, Footnote 26). Bedford County Lieutenant John Piper had given Council a plan by 1778 proposing enlisting men for nine months; he was refused, claiming that it exceeded his authority. [4] Earlier, in Bedford County, Woods and Smith (Section 6, Footnote 18) proposed the formation of ranging companies, though militia "ranged" from place to place.

> "...A small number of select men would be of more real services to guard the frontiers than six times that number of People unused to arms or the woods...Suppose there were orders given to raise about 100 Rangers under the command of spirited officers who were well acquainted with the woods and the Indians and could take them in their own way...." [5]

Except for taking the Indians in their own way, this was exactly what John Butler was working on (Section 5) while Smith and Woods were writing the above quote. The first words of this quote were nearly Colonel Hunter's thoughts (Section 6, Footnote 26). The Supreme Executive Council curtly dismissed Bedford County's proposals, via Smith and Woods, in November 1777, citing that raising soldiers outside the militia system and the regular Continental service would threaten the principles of liberty. They furthermore stated that since the militia law enacted in March 1777 does not mention any units with the word "ranger", such units could not be raised. No law, no unit. (Such are the beginnings of entrenched bureaucracy: Administration of the status quo becomes an end unto itself, regardless of the fact that the problems encountered might require new solutions.)

Washington perceived the need for copying the tactics of the various tribes and Loyalist partisans. And so did Reed. In a fascinating letter in the Pennsylvania Archives, Reed writes to his frontier county lieutenants:

> "On the _____ Inst., after several Conferences with a Committee

of Congress on the Defense of the Frontiers, the House of Assembly resolved to commit the whole Business to the Supreme Executive Council, who were to act in Concert with Congress & Gen. Washington on this important Business. Upon this, as Conference by Letters is very tedious & unsatisfactory, the Presid. [i.e., Reed] proposed to go to the camp & confer with the Commander in Chief in person, which he has accordingly done very much to his & our satisfaction. The General expressed his full sense of the Importance, Necessity & Duty of taking the most vigorous and speedy measures for the Support & Protection of the Frontiers. Such Parts of the Plan as are not necessarily kept secret in order to be more effectually executed we cheerfully communicate to you....It is also conslused to raise 5 companies of Rangers, making 380 men in the whole, to whom such Encouragement will be given....But we are further to acquaint you, that these are only Parts of the System; for it is fully determined to penetrate into the Indian Country,...& by a seasonable, vigorous stroke make them feel the weight of American Arms." [6]

In these secret conferences were the decisions to create the Sullivan & Brodhead expeditions as well as the creation of five companies of Pennsylvania rangers.

Out of these deliberations came several resolutions. The Continental Congress, in its minutes of February 25th, 1779, authorized the state of Pennsylvania to raise five companies of rangers for the protection of its frontiers. The following provisions were also stipulated: [7]

* Company size: 73
* Command structure:
  Captain (one)
  Lieutenant (two)
  Sergeant (four)
  Corporal (four)
  Drummer (one)
  Fifer (one)
  Private (sixty)
* Support staff for all five companies:

    Pay master (one)
    Deputy Commissary, Masters (quarter: one)
* Officers to be appointed by the Supreme Executive Council of Pennsylvania
* The Supreme Executive Council was urged, if felt necessary, to apply to the Pennsylvania legislature for an enabling law to make drafts upon the militia for men.
* Terms of service: nine months
* Bounty for enlistment: $100.00
* Pay: equivalent to Continental Line
* Requirements: Each man was to provide himself, at his own expense, with arms and clothing.

To implement this, the Pennsylvania General Assembly enacted such legislation, as reflected in its minutes of March 29, 1779, with these changes: [8]
* The state would furnish or pay each man for:
(a) Shoes, or six pounds in lieu of
(b) Hunting shirt, or 4 pounds, 10 shillings in lieu of
* The state would reimburse each man who used his own blanket in the amount of one pound, ten shillings.
* The state would reimburse each man who used his own arms and accoutrements in the amount of two pounds, ten shillings.
* Any man who lost his arms and accoutrements in the ranger service would be reimbursed in accordance with the resolutions of Congress of January 29, 1776. The Supreme Executive Council was authorized by the Assembly to ascertain the value of a man's arms so lost.

In public administration, it is one thing to authorize and enact legislation. It is another matter to implement it. The two may not look the same. Thus it was in the Revolution. The companies never achieved full muster. From the safety of a city on the east coast, a Continental Congress and/or state legislator saw the value of a drummer and fifer in each ranger company. Thank goodness for the men that this was never implemented. Unfortunately, however, neither were matters like pay and full company rosters.

Nevertheless, these acts by the Continental Congress and the Pennsylvania legislature conclusively prove that ranger companies existed in the state service; and that they were structured and designated as a military unit different from the Pennsylvania militia. They, with the militia, were to address the problems of frontier defense.

Washington was already discharging recuperating wounded officers and others whose regular term of enlistments were up to go home and help assist frontier defense. Such Northumberland County line officers included John Brady, who would be killed in April 1779 in a loyalist ambush near Muncy. His son, James, was scalped on the Loyalsock Creek and lived five days at Sunbury in August 1778 (the same "patriot", James Smith, was present each time). John's other son, Samuel Brady, would become the famous (in annals of border warfare) ranger captain of Westmoreland County. Such Northumberland County officers also included Hawkins Boone, cousin of Daniel Boone, who would be killed at the Battle of Fort Freeland July 28, 1779, leading his men and Captain Thomas Kemplin's Rangers against an expedition of Butler's Rangers and Iroquois numbering approximately 200. In attempting to rescue the women and children at Fort Freeland, approximately half of Boone's men were killed and scalped.

John's brother Sam, a ranger in Captain Thomas Kemplin's company, was also at Fort Freeland. Determined not to be made prisoner, he ran, pursued across open fields. He stopped and turned upon two Indians. He aimed and fired, killing one on the spot. The remaining one was running away, with Brady yelling after him words to the effect, "I'm Brady!" [9]

In the west, Brodhead, Commander of the Western Department stationed at Fort Pitt, saw the need for adopting Indian warfare tactics. In our 20th century, these tactics would be considered guerilla warfare. He took his 8th Pennsylvania Regiment of the Continental Army, recruited on Pennsylvania's frontiers, and created rangers. By April 15th, 1779, Brodhead wrote to President Reed: [10]

> "I have ordered ranging parties to cover them [Westmoreland County inhabitants] and drive out the Indians, and to intercept

such as may hereafter approach; this plan appears to me from
a considerable share of experience to be the most eligible, until
I am furnished with a supply of provisions [the garrison at Fort Pitt
was down to three days meat supply at this time]...to enable us to
attack some of their Towns."

Brodhead placed Samuel Brady, the son (not the brother of)) John Brady (see above) as over all commander. His specific orders included: [11]
* scouting the Allegheny Branch
* giving warning of approach of hostile parties
* pursuit of marauding bands

Brodhead had his rangers dress like Indians. [12] One of his men described their dress:

"Declarant states that in obedience to the order of said Captain
Brady, he proceeded to tan his thighs and legs with wild cherry and
white oak bark and to equip himself after the following manner, to
wit, a breechcloth, leather leggins [Figure 7.1.], moccasins and a cap
made out of a racoon skin with the feathers of a hawk, painted after
the manner of an Indian warrior. His face was painted red with three
black stripes across his cheeks, which was the signification of war.
Declarant states that Captain Brady's company was about sixty-
four in number, all painted after the manner aforesaid. " [13]

Brady fought along side his Delaware allies. The Delaware on the Muskingum were the only ones to maintain their neutrality, as other Indian nations, including the Shawnee, Wyandot, and Iroquois, sided with the British. In order to solicit their support in a potential offensive against Detroit, the rebellious colonies entered into a treaty with them in 1778. It was not until February, 1781, that the Delaware joined the other Indian nations in fighting. Even by 1779, various Delaware bands or individuals would raid the settlements. Thus here, too, Indian fought Indian, as the Delaware served Brodhead as scouts and traveled with the rangers. [14] A young Delaware chief, Nanowland, especially distinguished himself in combat to Brodhead, who recommended him and Brady to General Washington:

Figure 7.1. Breech Clout and Leggings.

> "Captain Brady fell in with 7 Indians...about 15 miles above Kittanning where they had chosen an advantageous situation for their camp....[B]y the break of day he attacked them and killed the Captain who was a notorious warrior of the Muncy [Delaware] nation and mortally wounded most of them. Capt. Brady retook six horses, the two prisoners, the scalps, and all the plunder which was considerable, and the six guns and everything else the Indians had except their Breech Clouts. Capt. Brady and most of his men acted with great spirit and intrepidity, but it is confest that the young Delaware Chief Nanowland (or George Wilson) distinguished himself on this enterprise...." [15]

Brodhead would, later in the war, recommend to Washington that Brady be promoted. [16]

There were at least three other ranger companies operating in Westmoreland County. One of these, Captain Thomas Stockley's company, was wiped out of existence in August, 1782. [17]

Northumberland County organized its first ranger company in the spring of 1779, financed by the state of Pennsylvania. Its company was that of Captain Thomas Kemplin, who fought with Boone at Fort Freeland (Footnote 17). A roster of this company of sixteen men, excluding Kemplin, includes: [18]
* 12 farmers
* 1 barber
* 1 tailor
* 1 scholar
* 1 gentleman

Their average height: approximately 5'8". Their average age: 26 years, 5 months. This includes 4 men aged 40 and one aged 45. So much for the image of the rugged ranger.

Organized for the first time in the spring of 1779, this unit engaged Butler, the Iroquois, and British regulars at Fort Freeland (Footnote 9) against overwhelming numbers; against a highly skilled enemy possessing a military tradition. If you, the reader, ever visit the site of Fort Freeland, near Warrior

Run Church, remember these men. Most, if not all of them, fought here. Traces of honor exist here, though no monument does. By the latter part of 1779, in 1780, 1781 and 1782, ranger companies of Northumberland County were the first line of defense after the disbursement of the population and subsequent disorganization of the militia. [19]

Bedford County also had ranger companies. Its first company, organized in 1779, was under the command of Thomas Cluggage, brother of Robert Cluggage, the commander of Fort Roberdeau. Their numbers were 3 officers and 43 rank and file. [20] One of these men, Luke Tipton, described his daily duties while stationed at Fort Roberdeau.

> "...[O]ur daily duty was to parade at the sound of Reveille on the parade ground and then get our breakfast and then prepare for a day or two scout chasing the Indians and Tories, sometimes after them and sometimes they after us." [21]

Pennsylvania ranger companies as described above, with the exception of Brady's rangers under Brodhead at Fort Pitt, differed in structure from Butler's. Butler's Rangers had a central chain of command emanating from their commander, Butler. In Pennsylvania, these ranging companies, though organized, supplied and paid by the state, were under the direct command of the local county lieutenant (Section 6) of the particular county: Westmoreland, Bedford and Northumberland; and later Washington, which was formed from Westmoreland County late in the war.

The author has found ranger companies performing the following duties:
(1) Offensive operations:
* acting as scouts, flank guards and guides
* guarding supplies en route to Sullivan's army (Kemplin's company)

(2) Defensive operations:
* constructing forts
* serving as the garrison of a fort
* guarding harvesters
* guarding prisoners

* "ranging" between forts
* gathering intelligence while scouting
* taking prisoners, equipment and supplies
* rescuing prisoners taken by the enemy
* breaking up raids heading into the settlements
* serving as the garrison of a fort and protecting the fort in case of attack

The highest ranking officer in any company was the captain. A company might have one or more lieutenants. One or more sergeants and ensigns comprised the noncommissioned officers, and privates the rank and file. Captain Thomas Robinson's company of Northumberland County also had a surgeon on its roster. The company, with this command hierarchy, served as the basis of organization.

Tours of enlistment varied. For Cluggage's Rangers, it was nine months; another time, three months. [22] These tours of duty took place usually during the spring, summer and fall, when Indian raids would be most active (another connotation to the term, "Indian Summer"). In the winter months, they would be quartered at some garrison until becoming active in the spring. If supplies and pay were scarce, they would be disbanded altogether. The man whose enlistment exceeded nine months was the exception. [23]

His uniform would generally consist of moccasins, breech clout, leggings, hunting frock or shirt, and cap - felt or leather (see also the description of Brady's men). At the Fort Augusta Museum, there is an original receipt signed by Captain Thomas Robinson for 29 pairs of moccasins for his troops. Like John Butler, the captains would encourage their men to have rifled guns, preferably their own. Robinson's Rangers of Northumberland County may have been more similar in their uniforms, for a warrior described the field dress of Major Moses Van Campen: a suit of bottle greened turned with red, including a large cap with a part white, part black cockade, with a feather in the top.[24]

Rev. Joseph Doddridge describes the frontier hunting shirt as follows:

"The hunting shirt was universally worn, this was a kind of loose frock, reaching halfway down the thighs with large sleeves, open before and so wide as to lap over a foot or more when belted." [25]

To the outer belt would go the scalping knife and the tomahawk. On a prolonged scout one would need a knapsack - a backpack with two shoulder straps; for short patrols, perhaps a haversack slung over one shoulder. Accompanying him would be his hunting bag containing rifle flints, a priming powder flask or horn, perhaps a compass and shot bag (containing musket balls). Perhaps he would have a canteen. At any rate, he would need a powder horn, patch knife, and patches for his rifle or smoothbore musket. In addition, he might have flint and metal to strike a fire, spare leather hides, and food (such as parched corn).

Pay varied from company to company and from year to year. Private Luke Tipton, in April 1779 , was given $60.00 bounty and $8.00 per month. [26] In February 1781, the Supreme Executive Council established a uniform pay scale for recruitment purposes: Non-commissioned officers and privates: 6 specie. [27] Pennsylvania issued a series of paper money, but these issues in the Revolution depreciated rapidly. This type of currency was undervalued and continued to depreciate until such time it was entirely out of circulation. By August 1781, one pound of "hard currency" or specie was equivalent to a five or six pound note. [28] Generally, pay for a ranger and bounty enlistment was less than either the Continental Line or the militia. [29]

To help compensate, aid was at least offered to Northumberland County. On April 8, 1780, the Pennsylvania Supreme Executive Council authorized the County Lieutenant of Northumberland County (Colonel Samuel Hunter) to offer an award of $1500.00 for each white prisoner, operating in active service with the Indians, and/or Indian prisoner; and an award of $1000.00 for each Indian scalp. [30] Whether this was formally offered to other frontier counties or only proposed (Footnote 16, Section 4) cannot to date be ascertained.

However, Pennsylvania's finances were strained to the breaking point for several reasons:
* She had to defend both her frontiers and eastern border from

invading British armies.
  * She had to furnish supplies to Washington's army, which also spent one winter at Valley Forge upon her soil, including wagons, homes, etc.
  * The state was the residence of the Continental Congress, along with its aides.
  * Prisoners of war were garrisoned in Pennsylvania.
  * She furnished material for the Sullivan expedition.
  * The occupation of Philadelphia by British forces curtailed potential resources.

If the Supreme Executive Council resolved to pay a particular company, the order would have to go through several channels. An order would be drawn on the state treasurer for a sum of money. This order would then be drawn in favor of an individual in a particular county, which would in turn be paid to the county lieutenant, who would pay the captain, and then in turn the rangers of his company. Provisions would follow the same procedures, given the request, through contractors in each county. At times, various individuals would directly supply the company with both pay and provisions and would be reimbursed through the state government. [31]

Lower pay and recruitment bounty, inadequacy of provisions, and multilayered chain of command hurt ranger effectiveness. Given the nature of the service, calling for mobility and surprise, their pay and supply system was anything but mobile. This hampered recruitment and the filling of company rosters. Local authority, under a county lieutenant, created conflicts of command structure, particularly between Brodhead and Archibald Lochry, County Lieutenant, Westmoreland County. Short time periods of enlistment created turnover and recruitment problems. Desertions for all these reasons were common. [32] Skill level in a company had to be affected by constant turnover and the need to recruit. Short terms of duty, even though greater than the militia (two months) had to have had an impact upon discipline.

In addition to the above problems, the ranger also encountered these:
  * The nature of frontier warfare (Section 5)
  * The more skilled opponent: the Tory ranger and his Indian ally

* The rapid need to match that skill level as quickly as possible in order to survive
* The problem of locality which the militiaman also experienced: Would he, the ranger, serve away from his family for an extended period of time (a longer period than that of the militia)?

It is no wonder that so few enlisted in this service. (See Figure 7.2.)

Figure 7.2:

> **Pennsylvania Ranger Recruitment Oath - 1780**
>
> "I ___ having been duly enlisted in the service of the state of Pennsylvania in the company of rangers commanded by Capt. ___ do promise to be true & faithful to the said state, agreeable to the terms of my enlistment and to be obedient to my Superior Officers. So help me God."

Contained in: "Instructions to Recruiting Officers, 1780" (Endorsed June 2, 1780 via Supreme Executive Council of Pennsylvania.). PA Archives, First Series, Vol. 8., p.291. Given to author by R. Emerson, Board of Directors, Fort Roberdeau Association; and Executive Director, Railroad Museum of PA.

Section 8:
Prelude to an Ambush
(Patriot Forces)

February, 1781, found John Boyd as newly commissioned captain of a ranging company formed for Bedford County, hereafter called Captain John Boyd's Bedford County Rangers. This company's existence can be traced back to a resolution of the Pennsylvania General Assembly, enacted February 21, 1780, creating the company. The Supreme Executive Council, in February 1781, authorized the appointment of Boyd to this position. [1]

Boyd's brother William had been killed as a lieutenant in the battle of Brandywine, PA, in 1777. In 1779, his other brother, Thomas, also a lieutenant, was captured and tortured to death during Sullivan's expedition. [2] John Boyd himself was a captain of the 3rd Regiment, Pennsylvania Line, Continental Army, by August 1777. He was a veteran of the battles of White Plains, Stony Point, Brandywine, and Germantown (the latter two fought in eastern Pennsylvania). [3] Prior to the war he lived in Northumberland County, at Northumberland. [4]

Spring, 1781, found Boyd recruiting, building up his company and guarding the frontier for seasonal anticipated troubles with Indian raids. His first lieutenant, Richard M. Johnson, was on recruiting duty in Cumberland County; and had secured several recruits in that county (in now Armagh Township, Mifflin County). [5]

On June 1st, word reached Boyd (who was possibly at Bedford) that Indians had crossed the Allegheny Mountains. Boyd decided to engage them. Accompanied by eight rangers, [6] he started north from Bedford, recruiting volunteers along the way. His destination was the Frankstown Blockhouse, built in 1780 and very near Fort Fetter, which was Michael Fetter's barn, a fortified barn. Fort Fetter was constructed in 1777. This blockhouse, the first at Frankstown, was also known as the Frankstown Fort. [7]

Volunteers (from the militia, on 60 day tours of duty; settlers; and/or any soldiers of the Continental Line on leave) joined him either initially at Bedford or en route to the Frankstown Fort (the blockhouse). These men included, but were not necessarily limited to, the following men: [8]

>Captain Richard Dunlap (or DeLapt) (Bedford County militia)
>Captain Samuel Moore (Bedford County militia)
>Captain William McDaniel (most likely Cumberland County militia)
>Lieutenant John Cook (12th Pennsylvania Regiment, Continental Line)
>Lieutenant George Smith (Bedford County militia)
>Lieutenant Harry Woods (militia: most likely Bedford County)
>Privates:
> James Henry (Bedford County militia)
> Horatio Jones (Bedford County militia)
> Patrick McDonald (1st Pennsylvania Rifle Battalion, "Thompson's Riflemen," Continental Line - a volunteer while on leave)
> Adam Witmer (unknown military affiliation)
> Hugh Means (Bedford County militia)
> James Moore (Bedford County militia)
> Zadock Casteel (Bedford County militia, most likely)
> Henry Tatlinger (Bedford County militia)

George Harris and U.J. Jones, in addition to the aforementioned officers and privates, list twelve other men in the ranks. Perhaps these men joined the force at the Frankstown Blockhouse. They are: [9]

>James Somerville
>Two Hollidays (Harris lists Adam and William Holliday)
>Two Colemans (Harris mentions Thomas and Michael)
>Michael Wallick
>Edward Milligan
>Two Jones brothers (Harris cites George Jones and his brother)
>---Gray (first name unknown)
>---Beatty (first name unkown)
>---Johnson (first name unknown - listed only by Harris)

If County Lieutenant George Ashman was correct in his report to President Reed in regards to 25 volunteers, (see footnote 5), then the above listings approximate his numbers. Perhaps others joined as well (see below).

There is general concensus in the sources that Boyd had eight rangers from his company with him at Frankstown. Certainly not all his mustered men were present at Frankstown. Who were the rangers present at this skirmish? Hoenstein [10] lists First Sergeant Henry Dugan. This is corroborated by Whisker. [11] Of the other seven rangers, given Whisker's compilation, [12] these are very likely candidates who served as volunteers in addition to those listed above:

> Bates (Beates), David. Private, Boyd's Rangers. Wounded at Frankstown on June 3rd, 1781.
> Bodle, Abraham. Pensioner who declared he was in Boyd's Rangers and was wounded in the right thigh at Frankstown on June 3rd, 1781.
> Conrad, John. Killed in service with Boyd's Rangers, possibly at Frankstown June 3rd, 1781.
> Downey, John Sr. Listed as private, Boyd's Rangers, killed in action, possibly at Frankstown.
> Downey, John Jr. Whisker states that he escaped the massacre at Frankstown and that his last military service was in Boyd's Rangers.
> Fraser, Benjamin. Private, Boyd's Rangers. Whisker cites one source claiming that a Benjamin Fraser was killed at Frankstown.
> Gobel (Gabel), Stephen. Corporal, Boyd's Rangers. Wounded in right arm at Frankstown.
> Grimes, Torrence. Boyd's Rangers. Listed as killed near Frankstown.
> Livingston, Daniel. Listed as private, Boyd's Rangers; taken prisoner at Frankstown, June 3, 1781.
> Martin, Joseph. Listed in Boyd's Rangers, killed in service, possibly at Frankstown.
> Murphy, Henderson. Killed at Frankstown June 3rd, 1781. Likely in Bedford County militia.
> Nicholas, Michael. Killed in action, possibly at Frankstown on June

     3rd, 1781.
  Tucker, William. Listed as killed in service with Boyd's Rangers,
    possibly at Frankstown, June 3, 1781.

It is possible that others not on the above list were serving at Frankstown and were not casualties. Regardless of service, if these 14 men were all present at Frankstown and several of them were rangers, then the additional seven from the last listing would place Boyd's force at no less than 42:
  * 9 Rangers, including Boyd and Dugan
  * 26 volunteers, from the first 2 lists
  * 7 additional, from this last listing.
British reports from the battle state they engaged a force equal to theirs. They, the British force, numbered approximately 40 men. [13]

The men who did not volunteer to serve with Boyd were units of the Cumberland County militia stationed at Fetter's Blockhouse. [14] They numbered approximately 70 men under command of a Colonel Albright and a Captain Young. [15] Jones states that this militia's primary duty was to guard the northwest Allegheny Mountain gaps and combat any Indian raiders before they reached the settlements. However, according to Jones, they were idle and inefficient. [16] Emerson states that the unwillingness to assist Boyd may have been due to reluctance to weaken the blockhouse's garrison or to not risk leaving the safety of the fort [17]. Hoenstein states that these militia had only a few days left to serve in their tour of duty; therefore, they would not risk their lives. He further states that they were probably ordered to stay in the fort [18] (by whom it is unclear - perhaps by Col. Albright, perhaps by the county lieutenant). Both Jones and Harris report [19] that (either Saturday, June 2nd, the day before the battle, or very early Sunday morning, June 3rd), Col. Albright was offered command of the men but he refused. Also, according to Harris, at least some of his men wished to join Boyd but he would not allow his men to leave the fort.

One of the volunteers, as stated above, was Horatio Jones. Jones was 17 1/2 years old by June 1st. His father, William, was a gunsmith and believed in the value of being physically fit. Jones became adept at wrestling and was a strong runner. When Horatio volunteered, his father objected, believing him too young to be furnishing his scalp as a trophy for some warrior. Given his self confidence in himself, he disobeyed. He also thought it cowardly not to answer the call. [20]

At Fetter's Blockhouse, Boyd's intent was to remain there on Sunday, June 3rd, and then take the Kittanning Path through the Kittanning Gap toward Pittsburgh, then cut southeast back home via Bedford. [21] (Section 10, Figure 10.1)

On Saturday, June 2nd, two scouts came to Fetter's, reporting that they had come across a recently abandoned Indian encampment near Hart's Sleeping Place. Their fires were still burning. Given the number of bark huts, the scouts estimated a party of 25-30. Boyd's men were confident of meeting them before they reached the settlements. They felt, given their experience with Indians, that they would not venture into the settlements until the next day. Thus, they could march and meet them near the mouth of the Kittanning Gap. [22]

They did not know their enemy.

Indian encampment.

Section 9:
Prelude to an Ambush
(Tory Forces)

Early in the spring of 1781, Captain Hendrick Nelles and his company of Butler's Rangers were ordered by Colonel John Butler to the Genesee River in western New York. Nelles and his company took up residence in the Seneca (Iroquois) village at Gah-ne-ya-de-o, on the east bank of the Genesee (Caneadea, the white corruption of the name, across the river from present-day Caneadea, NY). There, Captain Nelles took an Indian wife and set up housekeeping. Fulfilling his duty to the ranger corps but not wishing to take up a long forest march that time of year (or perhaps he lost some of his military edge by becoming a newlywed), he ordered his son who was with him, Lieutenant Robert Nelles, to lead an expedition to Pennsylvania. [1]

Lt. Nelles was specifically ordered to cut off continental troops passing between the Ohio and Susquehanna Rivers. Captain Nelles implored the Seneca, and perhaps other Iroquois warriors, to join his son. [2]

One Seneca family living below Caneadea on the west side of the Genesse at Ah-wes-coy had implored one of the Seneca chiefs, Do-eh-saw (meaning "one who propels or pushes himself, such as the strength of a beast of burden"; English name, Jack Berry, a half-breed son of a white trader) to bring back a captive - the youngest they might take. This white youth was to replace her son who was killed in battle with the whites. [3]

With Nelles went a squad of men and Iroquois warriors totalling about 40 men. [4] Besides Do-eh-saw, there was another subchief, or sachem, Hah-yen-de-seh (meaning "Dragging Wood" or "Hemlock Carrier") from Caneadea. This chief's father's white name was Hudson. Since he was a known warrior and military subchief, he was called "Captain Hudson". Hah-yen-de-seh inherited this "unofficial title" via the former military sachem, who was friends with a white family named Hutson or Hudson. [5] Thus in local American histories regarding Frankstown, this chief, Hah-yen-de-seh, is also called Hutson. [6] He was the son of this older military sachem. [7] Another subchief who accompanied Nelles was Gah-nee-songo (meaning "fond of berries"), also of Caneadea. The British called him Shongo. He was known to possess great physical strength. [8] Also on the expedition were several Indian warriors and women. [9]

Their route to the Juniata settlements is described by Harris: [10]
- * Beginning early in May, 1781, from Genesee through the Chautauqua Valley (New York) via the "Niagara Trail"
- * Through the Chautauqua Valley, moving southeast to the Canisteo River
- * Down the Canisteo to the Tioga River
- * From the Tioga River to Pine Creek (Ti-a-dach-ton, which was also a name used by earlier 18th century writers for Lycoming Creek) [11]
- * From Tiadachton Creek to the West Branch of the Susquehanna River (called by the Indians *Otzinachson*, meaning demon's den: where the evil spirits hold revels [12]).

They then marched through the forest trails and set up, as per Indian custom, base camp. Here stayed their supplies and the women. This base camp was within two days of Bedford. [13]

From this base camp, the joint Tory-Iroquois expedition advanced to the Juniata, intending to intercept troops moving on the Juniata River and/or attack some of the local forts. [14] Shongo led a band of warriors down the Juniata; but he apparently heard of the number of troops gathering at the Fetter Blockhouse. He reversed direction and quickly moved back upstream to join Hudson who, according to Harris, had built a temporary advanced camp at Hart's Log (now Alexandria, PA). [15]

From this advance camp, (either at Hart's Log or Hart's Sleeping place - see footnote 15), the expedition commander or the two aforementioned Indian chiefs sent scouts to watch the garrison at Fetter's. These Indian or ranger scouts apparently discovered Boyd's scouts, who had discovered the advance camp. They, the Indian/ranger scouts, did not give their presence away but reported back. That night (Saturday, June 2nd), in council, the rangers and Indians decided to lay an ambush the next morning, Sunday, June 3rd, at a place on the river. [16]

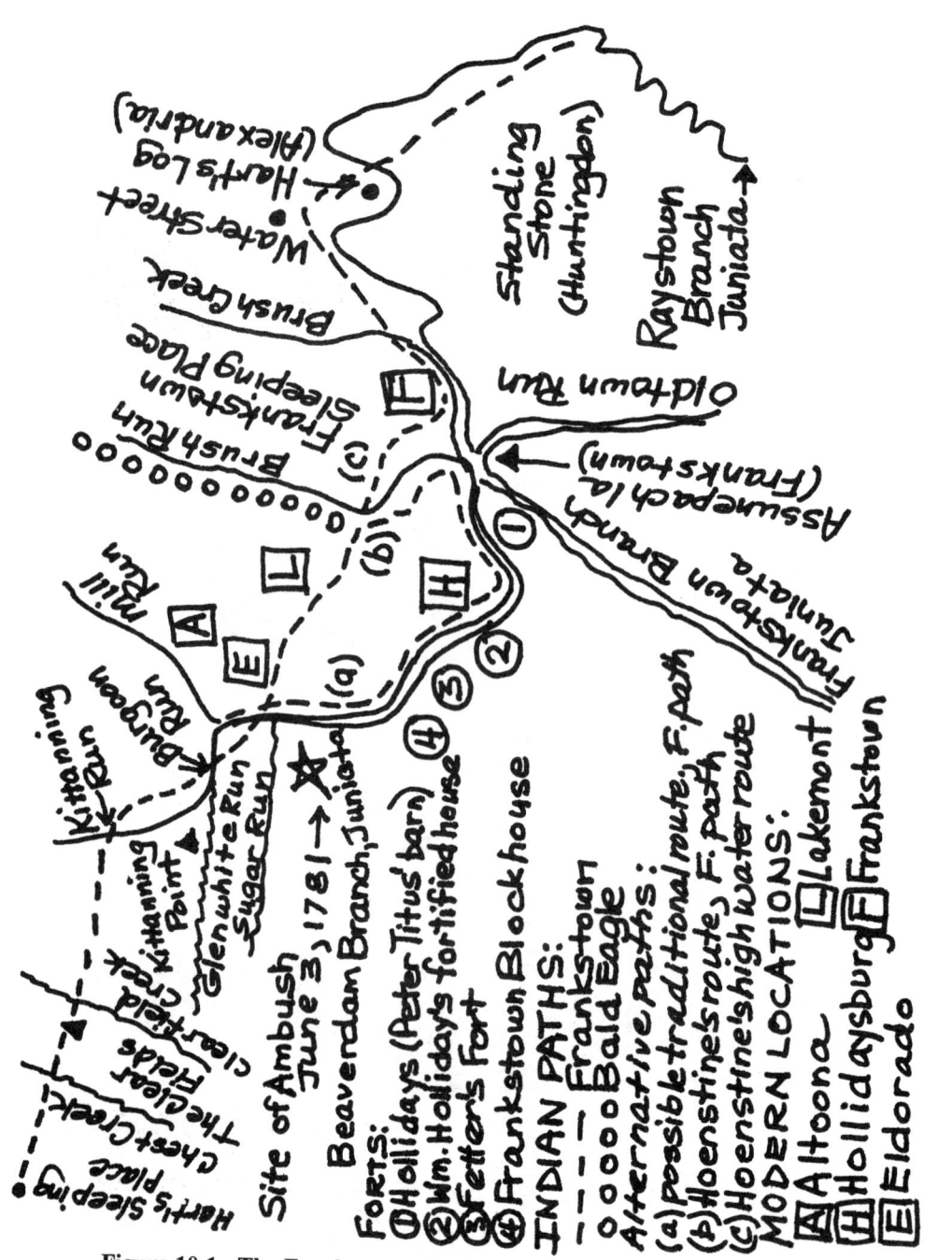

Figure 10.1. The Frankstown Path. (Note: the area around Hollidaysburg is purposely enlarged to show detail.)

Section 10:
We Who Stood, We Who Fell

Combat. Large or small, battle or ambush, it is the flashpoint, the horrific culmination of a chain of events, often seemingly disparate. It is also the beginning to sequel chains of events, often apparently unrelated, that forever end and/or sear, maim, change the lives of those engaged and those relating to them. As such, it is never an isolated act. Thus, at Frankstown, this Sunday, June 3rd, 1781.

The Indian Path, the Frankstown Path, was to play a major role in shaping the events leading to combat (Figure 10.1). It originated at Paxtang (Harrisburg) and made its way west and northwest. From Standing Stone (Huntingdon, PA) the path left the Frankstown Branch of the Juniata River. Traveling northwest, south of the river, it came to Harts Log (Alexandria, PA) after fording the river. From Hart's Log, the path followed the river on the north bank and came to Water Street (the present town). At Water Street the path travelled southwest, on the west side of the river, crossed over a shoulder of Canoe Mountain and came down near the mouth of Canoe Creek. Continuing southwest, it once again met the Juniata at the mouth of Brush Creek (Frankstown, PA); past a site southwest of modern Frankstown, called Frankstown Sleeping Place, and recrossed the Juniata to the original Frankstown (the Indian village of Assunepachla) which was situated on the south side of the river at the mouth of Oldtown Run, and across the mouth of the Beaverdam Branch of the river. [1]

West of Assunepachla, the Frankstown Path is known as the Kittanning Path. This path's culmination was the former Indian Village of Kittanning, destroyed by Col. John Armstrong's 1756 expedition in the French and Indian War. There were perhaps three branches in the Altoona-Hollidaysburg area [2]. One local historian cited by Wallace, Floyd Hoenstein, believed that the regular path, opposite the Indian village on the west side of the river, continued west on the north side of the Beaverdam Branch but left it very quickly to follow (different from Brush Creek, above) for about half a mile north; then it turned northeast to a fork in the path one-half mile below present Lakemont. From here, the path travelled northwest to present-day Eldorado. [3]

This was the regular route. In times of high water, according to Hoenstein, the path from Frankstown Sleeping Place cut over a high pass in the hills to reach Brush Run, one-half mile above its mouth. (This refers to the aforementioned forks.) [4] One of these forks was the Bald Eagle Path beginning here and running to the Bald Eagle's Nest (a former Delaware [Munsee clan] Indian village at the site of Milesburg, PA). [5] The other fork alluded to was, the author believes, the regular route of the Frankstown Path.

Wallace also cites another local tradition for the regular route of the path. Instead of travelling north up Brush Run, it continued to present-day Hollidaysburg, to where Allegheny Street enters it, then turned north to Eldorado. [6]

From Eldorado, the Frankstown Path changed direction, veering west along the south bank of Burgoon Run, crossing it to the north bank at the present site of the Allegheny Reservoir. It passed underneath the site of the railroad where it begins the Horseshoe Curve, below Kittanning Point (called this by the early traders using this path). From here the path traveled north, up Kittanning Run for one and a half miles. After climbing the ridge, it left Blair County, crossing into Cambria County. It continued northwest from the mountain ridge, descending to a clearing called "The Clear Fields" (approximately three-fourths mile southwest of present-day Ashville) - an Indian encampment located at the confluence of Clearfield Creek and Beaverdam Run (not to be confused with the Beaverdam Branch of the Juniata). [7]

From here, running northwest, the Kittanning Path ran past or through the present villages of Chest Springs and Eckenrode Mill, where it crossed Chest Creek and continued northwest, passing the present town of Hastings to the south. Before it reached Hastings, it came to the site known as Hart's Sleeping Place. [8]

Recall from Section 8 that Boyd's scouts had discovered the site of the advanced

Recall from Section 8 that Boyd's scouts had discovered the site of the advanced Indian Camp. Recall from Section 9 that Nelles' scouts had discovered Boyd's scouts and were going to ambush Boyd's expedition. From near their advanced Indian encampment, probably at Hart's Sleeping Place, travelling at night or very early Sunday morning along the Kittanning Path before daybreak June 3rd, Nelles' party broke camp. They made their way east over the Allegheny Mountain front, below Kittanning Point, down Kittanning Run, following the trail parallel to Burgoon Run to its junction with the Beaverdam Branch. Here they left the trail and proceeded south. Most likely, by this time, advanced scouts were following Boyd's men as they left Fetter's Blockhouse that morning and were relaying intelligence back to Nelles' party. At any rate, they trailed past the mouth of Sugar Run and, 30 rods south of its juncture with the Beaverdam Branch (Figure 10.2.), set up their ambush. The major force of the ambush faced east toward the Beaverdam Branch. The site was south of Sugar Run and south of the Kittanning Path.

Sunday morning, June 3rd, Boyd's rangers and volunteers were up before daylight. [9] Excitement filled the air: a sense of heightened anticipation over the impending battle. After breakfast, they loaded their knapsacks [10] with five days provisions.

Their clothes were not standard uniforms but represented the frontier dress at this time: a cap, hunting frock, breeches or Indian style leggings and Indian style breech clout, and moccasins. The frock was enwrapped within an outer belt which held a tomahawk and/or hunting knife (or scalping knife). Besides the knapsack, there would be need for a canteen (tin or wooden - probably quart sized), powder horn, patch knife, priming powder horn, hunting bag, extra rifle flints, striker and flint for starting fires, perhaps sewing supplies, and food. Some men's moccasins were of hides with flaps shin-high, with long strings of hide about the ankles and shins to secure the flaps. Ideally, each was armed with a flintlock rifle and not a smoothbore musket. [11]

From Fetter's, they started north, along a path on the left side of the Beaverdam, marching single file - north toward the Kittanning Path. [12] Boyd posted no advanced scouts or flankers, apparently believing that the Indians were on the west side of the mountains. [13] He may also have felt

Figure 10.2. Ambush at Frankstown: June 3, 1781. Adapted from Robert L. Emerson, "Debacle on the Juniata: the Battle of Frankstown, 1781", *The Mansion*, (Blair County Historical Society: Altoona, PA), Vol. 8, No. 1, June 1981, 1.

invisible, [14] or that they were still too close to the fort (Fetter's) for any surprise attack to occur: no Indians would attack this close. [15] Captain Boyd led, followed by Sergeant Henry Dugan. Then came the volunteer officers, trailed by the other rangers and volunteers. [16]

Join in, reader. Allow yourself to drift.

As a new ranger recruit, you are not yet familiar with your fellow comrades-in-arms of this ranger company, let alone with all these new volunteer faces. What are their quirks in combat? How will they behave? Will they, as a body, instinctively follow orders in a crisis? Perhaps you have completed a 60-day militia tour of duty. Perhaps you have guarded harvesters or even helped garrison a fort. But have you ever fought before? Feel the early morning dew and streamlets soak your moccasins. Feel the weight of your pack.

Careful now. Don't clang your powder measure against your horn! Check your 'hawk again. Is the blade out from your body in case you fall or are pushed? Can you grab it easily and quickly unloosen the cloth or hides ensheathing it? Is your powder dry?

"Yeah, the plug's still in the horn. My G--, where's my priming horn? Yeah. In my hunting bag. Better unloosen its flaps, just in case. No. Don't want to spill it. How about the priming horn's plug. Knife. Can I reach and unsheath it? Try quickly. There. Should I put priming powder in my rifle's pan now? Save a few seconds. I've heard tell how the savages fight."

"What was that? Oh, blue jay. The h--- it was! Too big. Bear off the mountains. Maybe a buck."

Wood thrushes call through the fog. Wood warblers trill from the thickets about the Beaverdam, just to the right.

"Dugan's a vet. He's not scared. Boyd fought the British. Good men. What-!" [Movement on the left. A flash, and out of sight.] "Whatever it was, it's parallel to us. Birds still singing. Remember what Dugan said: even skulking savages scare birds."

"Heart's pumpin' now. Feet wet and cold now. Mocs. Check out the strings. Are my moc flaps in place? Lot of water to cross today before we hit the hills and my feet are already soaked. Wet leather's gonna be rubbin'. Wha-! Now what's them sounds? Chirps? Clicks? Again to the left. T'ain't no chirpin...!"

T'wern't no chirp you heard, reader. Those were the locking in place of flintlock triggers. For a split second, frozen in time, silence. Then almost simultaneously, the only sounds are the calls of frightened birds taking off, the cackling of the jay. Then a single pierced sharp verbal cry - followed by the flash of tiny fires. Then a tremendous CRACK! followed by stacatto cracks, intermingled with the shrill scalping cries of the Iroquois warriors and Nelles' rangers. Fury unleashed.

The ethereal shapes quickly take form. A black and red painted human is bounding straight at you, reader. The 'hawk poised above his head is about to be hurled at you while he's slinging a rifle in the other hand. Your sight encodes this. Amidst the din, you peripherally hear some shouts of command. Some are not in English. Another split second frozen in time.

"Too late for my rifle. Do I run? Do I reach for my 'hawk? My knife? Where's the 'hawk? It's out of the hand now! Pick it up! Duck! To the right!" -as it crashed into the oak you just leaped behind.

Choices. Your life is framed for eternity in split seconds. Each second is a lifetime of intense sensory overload. About you, men are screaming with sharp, searing pain produced by a lead ball. They discover spontaneously that they can't move and they fall down. The unmistakeable sharp splintering of human bone as a 'hawk finds its target. The screams of a wounded man being scalped alive.

"Do I fight it out here? He knows where I am. I can't load and fire in time. Do I run?"

You forget that the pack you're still wearing is dead weight. Thoughts, centered on survival, emotions and sensory stimuli intermix, speeding up yet transcending time, producing the peculiar stress of combat...

This attack was so sudden, seemingly so numerous (though the forces mathematically were about equal) that the rangers, militia and volunteers, unused to fighting as a unit to begin with, were thrown into immediate confusion. Each man fought individually or ran for his life. [17]

Boyd was up against not only Indians, skilled in their own methods of warfare, but also up against a lieutenant in Butler's Rangers and fellow rangers skilled in their own tactics. Two of these tactics were in operation here:
  * Ambush those wanting to ambush you.
  * Never get caught between an enemy and a stream.
Furthermore, they and their Indian allies were veterans, used to fighting together. Even as a unit, Boyd's Rangers were comparatively new; and only nine of this unit were on the field.

Horatio Jones (one of the volunteers listed in Section 8) was deafened by the firing and half blinded by the smoke, caught up in the frenzied rush of those fleeing. This burst of unleashed fury carried him into the middle of the river. No thoughts of valor here. He ran away from this hell, opposite it, splashing through the cold water to the opposite shore and straight up the bank. Two Indians suddenly appeared with leveled guns. He changed directions. They pursued him but didn't fire. He wheeled about, raised his rifle and fired. A spark, but no discharge! The priming powder was wet from the river. The rifle, useless. He whirled and ran, crossing the narrow valley between this side of the Beaverdam and a hill later known as O'Friel's Ridge. [18]
Jones ran up this hill.

The two warriors who had fallen flat when he "fired" now joined the chase, yelling in broken English to stop. Jones' one moccasin string was loose, catching in the shrubs. He fell. He tried to get up but his foot was caught. The two warriors were over him now. He sat still, very still, as much as his pounding heart would let him. Jones showed no resistance.

One of the warriors picked up Jones' rifle, removed the rifle flint and the wet powder, and handed the useless piece back to Jones. They took his knife and 'hawk, tethered him with a blanket, and motioned for him to get up. In broken English, one said he would make a fine Indian and complemented him on his running ability. Jones' life was forever changed, for one of these warriors was Do-eh-saw (Jack Berry, Section 9). [19]

Harry Woods, James Somerville and Michael Wallack (Section 8) also found themselves in the river. They splashed across and ran up the same ridge Jones had. Somerville trailed the others. Somerville's moccasin, too, became untied. He couldn't continue with it loose. Taking a chance, he stooped down to tie it. A warrior bounded at him with uplifted 'hawk.

Woods also stopped, perceiving Somerville in trouble. He turned and purposely aimed his empty rifle, knowing that he had shot it earlier when across the stream. The Indian, seeing the barrel aimed at him, leapt behind a tree. He peered out and recognized Woods. He yelled words to the effect, "I won't hurt you, Woods!"

It was Hudson (Section 9), the son of the chief who was friends with Woods' father. Woods, too, suddenly remembered. The three whites had come as close to Indians today as they cared to come. It was not yet time to recount childhood memories. The three whites ran up the ridge as fast as they could go and circled around to Fetter's. [20]

(Woods survived the war. Many years later, he lived in Pittsburgh. One day he was at the river bank when a canoe with Indians appeared. One jumped out and clasped his hand in a shake and said, to this effect, "Woods, that day at the Juniata, you ran like the devil." It was Hudson.) [21]

The two Jones brothers also ran. One reached Fetter's and reported a large force to Albright (Section 8). His brother couldn't keep up. The Coleman brothers, too, had survived the onslaught and discovered Jones lying behind a log, resting. One of the Coleman's said to get up and push on. Jones promised. Both Coleman's pushed on as quickly as possible to get to the fort. [22]

Was there any organized or individual resistance? It is hard to ascertain from this distance of time. The historian Jones states that Woods' rifle was the only one fired. [23] Hoenstein cites an interesting anecdote reported by Annie Gilchrist of Bedford. She stated that James Henry had told a friend of a premonition he had before the battle. In a dream, he was captured by the Indians. He then told his friend he would never surrender but fight to the end. Gilcrist, Hoenstein relates, stated that a search party later found Henry's body, mutilated, and five dead Indians about it. [24]

Captain Boyd was leading, out in front, at the initial volley. What attempts at resistance he himself made or ordered cannot be ascertained. However, it is known that he attempted to escape after the defeat and was wounded in the head with a tomahawk - receiving three gashes. He was taken prisoner. [25]

British sources state that Nelles' party had one killed and two wounded. [26] This gives some idea of the resistance they encountered. It is entirely possible that in the fog and melee of battle that "friendly fire" could have ensued.

Butler's Rangers in the field in 1781 may not have had the dress uniform ascibed to them (Section 4), thus blending in with Boyd's men. They could have all been dressed like their Iroquois allies. American historians writing about this battle never mention Tory rangers taking part. Nor does the primary source, George Ashman, County Lieutenant, Bedford County, in his report to Joseph Reed, President, Supreme Executive Council of Pennsylvania, 9 days after the ambush.[27] The amount of men wounded nor the nature of the wounds in Boyd's party does not, in and of itself, offer proof of resistance, as one historian has indicated. [28] For example, a tomahawk gash in the back shoulder as compared to the front has many different interpretations: grappling hand-to-hand combat; a warrior coming to the aid of another and striking his foe in the back; or receiving the wound while running away. Bullet wounds offer no proof of resistance. One may have been wounded in the first volley.

An historian must also ask, what about the possibility of Nelles embellishing his report by lowering his casualty figures, knowing that Indians will not write reports? The sounds of silence are deafening. In Ashman's report of Reed [29] there is no record of the militia relief party burying any enemy dead - not even one of finding fresh graves.

What about the prisoners of war taken? Do they mention enemy losses in their eye witness observations? Harris [30] states that Jones, after he had been made prisoner, observes about him several bodies of "rangers" and warriors. Since Harris, in his work, also calls Jones a ranger, is he, Harris, confusing militia, which Jones was, for rangers? Does Jones mean Boyd's rangers or Nelles' rangers? It is possible that Indian warriors were killed, for Harris also states Jones' recollections that the Indians carefully buried their dead in order to conceal them.

If correct, this offers the greatest proof of resistance by Boyd's men. It is possible that the militia relief party never discovered them. It is also possible that Jones was embellishing the resistance offered. As a prisoner of war and survivor of the war, Boyd has made no mention of resistance and he was the commander. Or, if he has, no evidence has survived or yet been discovered. To date, there is no evidence to corroborate Jones, through Harris. One has to ask what number did Jones mean when he used the word "several"? Finally, Ashman's report and Harris' account of Horatio Jones conflict with the Gilchrist anecdote regarding Henry, cited above.

(For a final word on the possibilities of organized resistance, the reader is urged to consult Section 11, especially footnote 22.)

The combat tactics employed by Nelles, Shongo and Hudson were those of ambush. Without any positive evidence to the contrary, the result was a rout. There was no pitched battle. There was no skirmish. At Bald Eagle Creek in April, 1782, Robert Nelles' tactics of ambush turned into a skirmish because organized resistance as a combat unit was offered immediately by Robinson's Rangers, under the command of Moses Van Campen. [31] Hence the importance of skill level and the experience of working together. Again, Boyd had only a part of his company of rangers with him in this debacle (as Emerson calls it [32]) and they were working with an assortment of individuals for the first time, probably at various levels of experience and skill.

An accurate assessment of the patriot casualties at Frankstown is impossible given the fact that no accurate listing of the men engaged was made; or, if made, has not survived or been discovered. It is possible that men were wounded and died somewhere in the forest after attempting to escape. Or that those wounded, and/or made prisoners, died later (Section 11).

Ashman [33] reports that Captain Young of the Frankstown garrison stationed at Fetter's immediately sent out a relief party from the garrison as soon as survivors reported what happened. This relief party, according to Ashman, found five wounded and ran across two unwounded. At the battle site, they found eight killed and scalped. Captains Boyd, Moore, and Dunlap plus six others were missing. Harris reports that Jones, as a prisoner, observed his enemy with nine scalps as trophies. [34] The historian Jones states that this relief party was sent out that same Sunday, commanded by Captain Young, whose purpose it was to bring in any survivors.

Historians have listed casualties at Frankstown as rangers, mistaking militia for rangers. Perhaps they have assumed that since Boyd was in over all command, all his men were rangers. Or, knowing the difference, they simply listed them as rangers because of Boyd's title. They only distinguish between volunteers and rangers. [36] However, as listed in Section 8, only nine rangers, including Boyd, were engaged in this battle.

Given this caveat, the interested reader can compare the following names taken from Hoenstein [37] to those units and individuals mentioned in Sections 8 and 11 as well as the numbers in Ashman's report (Pvt. designates private):

Dead:	Wounded:	Missing/Prisoners
Captain Richard Dunlap	Sergeant David Beate	Captain John Boyd
Captain William McDaniel	(or Beates; or Bates)	Captain Samuel Moore
Sergeant Torence Grimes	Corporal Stephen Goble	Lieut. John Cook
Pvt. John Conrad	Pvt. Abraham Bodle	Lieut. George Smith
Pvt. John Downey, Sr.	Pvt. Hugh Means	Sergeant Henry Dugan
Pvt. James Henry	Pvt. Adam Wimer	Pvt. Horatio Jones
Pvt. Henderson Murphy	(or Witmer)	Pvt. Patrick McDonald
Pvt. Michael Nicholas		
Pvt. John Thomas		
Pvt. William Tucker		
Pvt. Henry Tattinger		
(or Tatlinger)		

Dead: (cont'd.)
Pvt. ____ Jones
      (first name unknown)

On Monday Morning, June 4th, Captain Young again set a party out from Fetter's - this time to bury the dead. They were committed to the earth where they fell. Hopefully, the men dug deep graves for those they found. Hopefully, they did not simply cover the remains with stones, leaves and or bark in order to avoid the bodies becoming food for wolves. On Tuesday, Jones still sought his missing brother, the one resting by the log, the one told by one of the Coleman's to push on to the fort. All he found were the crushed remains of bones. [38]

By Spring, 1852, that interregnum between wars fought and gathering thundercaps of civil war, a farmer was plowing his fields - preparing the earth for the seeds of nourishment rather than feeding it past seeds of retribution. By the bank of the Beaverdam, his plow exhumed a skeleton - perfectly preserved and uncoffined. Examining it, he saw that a bullet hole had perforated its skull. [39]

Spring. This golden season with its suffusion of oozing life is in stark diametrical contrast to this dank symbol of death: this discovered skull and skeleton. What emotions the farmer felt are lost in time. What emotions do you have, reader, imagining this?

Be the farmer. Be not afraid. This scene, you and "it", portray the cycle of life. And in its silence, before turning to decay and ashes, before renourishing the earth for renewed life, this skeleton speaks to us.

Hold him in reverence, reader. Once, like you, he was teeming with hopes and aspirations and brimming with emotions. Friend or foe, victor or vanquished, it matters not. Regardless of his reasons for fighting here that Sunday in June, respect this warrior and what he represented. Listen. He speaks. The sounds of silence are deafening: "I am, who was here".

Section 11:
Aftermath

Though Captain Young of the militia did not serve in the debacle, he deserves credit for his leading the party that same day to bring in the wounded and the next day in leading the party to bury the dead. The Cumberland County militia at Fetter's, either through Col. Ashman or Captain Young, proceeded to prepare the fort for attack and sent out messengers to warn the settlements and other forts of the danger. [1]

County Lieutenant Ashman, in his report to President Joseph Reed, Supreme Executive Council of Pennsylvania, states that Young immediately sent him information on the calamity and that he, Ashman, was organizing a relief party for pursuit of the enemy. However, he reports that before he could do this, the enemy had returned over the Allegheny Mountains. Because of high water due to heavy rains, they could not be pursued. [2]

Bedford County was in a deplorable situation, according to Ashman. Ashman received word from Colonel Abraham Smith of Cumberland County that he had no orders to send Ashman any more militia. Ashman also stated to Reed that the Cumberland County militia already in Bedford County had only 2 more days of enlistment before their tour of duty expired; and that ammunition was nil to nonexistent. As for the settlements, they would be abandoned. He himself was moving his family to Maryland. [3]

Nelles, Hudson and Shongo, together with the whole force and prisoners and gathered materiel of war, prepared the night of the battle to return to their homes and headquarters. As can be seen from the casualty listing in Section 10, several of the officers were prisoners. A captive officer was worth more than a captive private; and prisoners were worth more than scalps when bartering with the British. [4] Perhaps the volley of first fire was not directed at those in the lead, thinking that they were officers.

However, Captain Dunlap was severely wounded as a prisoner. After marching several hours that Sunday, he was exhausted. Blows to prod him on failed to keep him moving. He was already straining under the booty he was forced to carry. Without warning, a warrior stepped behind him and buried his tomahawk deep into the back of his neck and pulled back, thus jerking the still-alive body over backwards. As Dunlap fell, the Indian quickly stripped him of his scalp. The party left his quivering body and pushed on. [5] The lesson was clear to the others: a wounded man, even an officer, would not hold up these raiders.

Initially, the prisoners were tethered with blankets about the legs. However, the blankets soon became saturated with wet grasses and greatly restricted their movements. These were removed before the afternoon. [6] In order to secure the captives at night, a tree was cut down. Notches were groved in the tree. Laying on the ground, the notches were matched to the prisoners' ankles, thus creating stocks. This was fastened to other newly-cut poles. A heavy cord or rope was then placed over the prisoners' bodies and under several warriors at each end. An active tug in attempting to escape and any given warrior would feel the cord move beneath him. [7]

That same afternoon, June 3rd, Nelles' party sent a messenger ahead to notify the base camp of its approach and with orders to prepare for immediate departure. That evening they reached this camp. Fearing pursuit, they soon pushed on, stopping only long enough for the women to finish packing. It was to be a night march. With the anticipation of battle, some of the prisoners had no sleep that Saturday night, prior to Sunday's ambush. All had now marched since sunrise Sunday, breakfast being their last meal. They had fought and been wounded in battle, captured, tethered, carried heavy loads, and now, barely able to navigate the paths in daylight, were to stumble along in the dark. Dunlap's lesson was fresh in their memories. They quickly discovered as well how rapid Nelles' Rangers and Iroquois marched. Early Monday morning, Nelles finally halted. All threw themselves down upon the damp earth. [8]

At daylight, they resumed. Now Nelles feared not a pursuit party from Bedford, but scouting patrols from the West Branch. [9] He expected attack at any time. For two days they moved, preserving strict silence, having no cooked food, no shelter, no fires, nor allowed any hunting. No gun was allowed to be discharged after the ambush. [10] By the third day, even the Indians were physically suffering. On this day they discovered a bear. Needing nourishment, they killed it. The prisoners were given the entrails and small pieces of raw flesh as their rations. They readily ate. [11]

Perhaps within a day or two more, they crossed the West Branch, near the mouth of Sinnemahoning Creek. Here they encamped, having discovered no sign of their enemies, and soon had meat. Among the prisoners was a man named Ross, [12] badly wounded. Boyd himself had lost a fair amount of blood. Ross couldn't travel any further. Here the Indians had him tortured to death; his body was stuck with numerous pitch pine splinters and fire applied. Boyd had been tied to a white oak sapling to witness this, and was told that his turn was next. [13]

Told to prepare himself for his "turn", Captain Boyd began to sing a Masonic song. The Indians, men and women, listened intently until he was done. At this moment, an elderly woman claimed Boyd as her son! The men did not interfere. Throughout the remainder of the journey into Canada, this Oneida Iroquois woman cared for him. [14] Such were the vagaries of the Iroquois mind to the frontier settler: fury or compassion? One never knew. [15]

From the Sinnemahoning, the war party crossed to the Tioga River, down the Tioga (perhaps by the Tioga Path, unless the water was high enough for rafts or canoes) to the mouth of the Cohocten, where existed an Indian village. It had a large, oddly painted, post standing in open land to depict an enemy. Hence the modern New York town, Painted Post. At night, the warriors from the raid danced around this post and recounted their exploits in front of the prisoners, including the display of their comrades' scalps. All had to remain silent. All knew not to display any signs of rage or all would be killed on the spot. [16]

From Painted Post, the party traveled up the Conestio Valley (probably via the Forbidden Path), through the Chatauqua Valley in Allegheny County, New York, to the Genesee River. They reached the Genesee villages of the Seneca on June 20th, on the east bank of the river, across from the probable village of Ah-wes-coy, where a squaw asked Do-eh-saw (Jack Berry) for capture of a white boy, and crossed the river at a ford to the village. [17]

One of the two warriors who had captured Jones was Do-eh-saw (Jack Berry), who told him prior to the Genesee crossing that he and the other prisoners would have to run the gauntlet in this village. It was the Indian custom to have the women and children vent their spite on the prisoners for revenge for those taken in battle. It also signified the prisoner's endurance and courage. [18] All had to encounter this, regardless of prior plans for adoption.

Before leading the raiding party across the river, Lieutenant Nelles addressed all prisoners that when reaching the other side, when given the word, they were to run for their lives and aim for the house on the hill displaying a white flag. (This was the long house, or council house, built by carpenters from Fort Niagara.) In the run, any person in the lines of Indians had the right to strike, wound, or kill them. If they reached the house, they would then be safe. They would be entitled to freely enter it and be immune from further punishment. Nelles added that he felt it proper to tell them this. [19]

In the run, Jones was behind Boyd, McDonald and Johnson. Do-eh-saw originally had shielded Jones and held him back to give the others a head start. This was meant as protection, since the lines' attention would be on the front runners. The above three had received many wounds and reached the house. Three or more young braves were standing by the door and attacked them, despite warning cries from the older warriors. One of these braves was named Wolf. He raised his sword, swung, and took off Johnson's upper head. Johnson's brains splattered on Jones' face. Wolf's "brave" comrades joined him, attacking Boyd and McDonald. Jones ran. One called Sharp Shins, threw an axe at Jones. (In later life Jones said he still heard the sound made by the whirling axe as it passed him.) Jones knew that if he got into the council house, it offered the best chance of survival even though the rules of the game had already been broken. He ran around a corner of the house. Closed. No door nor window. He ran from it, on a path, into a thicket of woods and in a clearing ran into the first house he found. It was the house of the squaw who had petitioned Do-eh-saw to give her a captive boy. Other squaws accompanied her and Jones, concealed by the blankets of the women, was led into the council house. Jones was safe. [20]

He found himself with the others, all having apparently survived, including somehow, Boyd and McDonald. That night, the village celebrated their return. Liquor from Niagara perhaps was the other excuse or provided the incentive to celebrate. The men freely indulged. Some of the women prudently remained sober and removed as many of the weapons as they could find. The debauchery continued long into the night. The prisoners, contained in the long house with male guards to protect them, shuddered. Soon drunken revelers beat down the door and rushed into the building, their fury beyond containing by mere mortals. Wolf and Sharp Shins were among them. They seized McDonald. He was to become their sport. Sharp Shins finally tomahawked him and chopped off his head and thrust a spear in it. The spear was stood on end and the warriors danced about the head. The men then rushed the council house, their fury but ignited. It was empty. The women had taken the prisoners away. In a sodden drunken stupor, these momentary impersonators of humanity gradually fell to the earth and slept where they lay. [21]

The following day, when the men's senses were recovered, the women restored the prisoners and the men's weapons. They convened in a stately council, hardly recognizable as the fiends of the night before. The warriors sat in a circle with the prisoners within it. Other men and the women and children were in the outer circle, beyond the warriors. Hudson rose and spoke to this effect: "Enough," he said. "Enough blood has been shed to atone for those killed." [22]

The council's task was to determine the disposition of the survivors. Do-eh-saw rose. He recounted the squaw's request to him, of Jones' fleetness afoot, of his courage and trustfulness displayed on the march home, of Providence leading Jones to the woman after the gauntlet. Silence. Gah-nee-songo (Shongo) arose. He said, in effect, "that his eyes and ears were now open. Now he truly heard. Now he truly saw. The Great Spirit had delivered Jones to them for a purpose. The Great Spirit would reveal this purpose in time. It was wise for his children to listen. The white boy was to remain." [23]

And so it was. The village council approved. Jones stayed and remained - voluntarily. A year later, he was to save the life of a celebrated Northumberland County ranger, Moses Van Campen (lieutenant, Captain

Thomas Robinson's Rangers), himself taken captive in a skirmish with Nelles and the Iroquois on Bald Eagle Creek (west of present-day Lock Haven, PA). He would not reveal Van Campen's identity, knowing the Iroquois would kill him if they discovered who he was. [24] Perhaps the Iroquiois would not consider it God's purpose to save an enemy; but Heaven's purposes are not constrained by earth bound consciousness.

Gah-nee-songo and Do-eh-saw did, however, foresee that this man had been saved for a purpose. Jones became an interpreter for the Iroquois. As interpreter, he took part in peace negotiations with the United States after the Revolution. He also rendered his services in land sales and court cases involving the Iroquois. [25] In grateful recognition to him and another interpreter, Jasper Parish, the Seneca deeded to them two square miles of land. This land later became part of Buffalo, New York. [27]

The other prisoners were taken to Niagara. The Oneida woman who saved Boyd's life on the Sinnemahoning and assisted in his rescue from the council house now accompanied him to Niagara. She also accompanied Boyd when he and the others were transported to Quebec via ship. [28] In Quebec, Boyd was placed in a hospital, under the care of a British surgeon. He rapidly recovered. He was turned out onto the streets of Quebec, penniless and friendless. Wandering, he came upon an Inn with the words "Masonic Inn" on the sign. Entering, he gave the sign of the Order to the proprietor. Boyd was taken in and cared for until exchanged. [29]

After the war, Captain Boyd did not forget this woman. He often sent her money and gifts. Once it was reported that he made a pilgrimage to her Indian home to thank her for saving his life. The captain died at Northumberland, PA, in 1831, at the age of 82. He was 32 years old while in command that Sunday so long ago, in the spring of his life. For those 50 years, the wounds to his head caused him to keep up a constant winking. [30]

CONCLUSION

Frankstown was not an isolated event. By analyzing Frankstown, one studies four distinct military commands operating on Pennsylvania's frontiers during the Revolution: the rangers - both (1) Tory loyalist and (2) Patriot; (3) the Pennsylvania militia and volunteer settlers and the frontier culture from which they came; and (4) the Iroquois. By assessing Frankstown, one discovers inextricable connections not only with the history of the Juniata Valley and Blair County (Pennsylvania), but also with the West Branch Valley of the Susquehanna (Pennsylvania) and New York state.

On its surface, Frankstown is simple. On its surface, it was an insignificant frontier ambush that "we", the patriots, lost. Within its anatomy, it is a complex web of life interconnecting seemingly disparate events, peoples, and persons. Individual lives were forever changed by the combat at Frankstown.

Frankstown teaches us that history is complex, not simple. As the Civil War historian Shelby Foote has stated, if you take the complexity out of history, you lose history. History then becomes simplistic platitudes. The American Revolution becomes stars and stripes paraded on the Fourth of July.

When we lose complexity, we lose history and the lessons it presents. Frankstown teaches us that life, consisting of seemingly disparate events, is in reality ecologically complex and interrelated. Touch one strand of the web of life and the whole web vibrates.

Frankstown reinforces important lessons to the student of military history:
* The importance of time in order to function as a unified command structure.
* The importance of time in gaining a level of experience and skill equivalent to, if not greater than, your enemy.
* Never underestimate your enemy. Know him and his tactics.

* Certain needs are constant, regardless of proximity to support and situation - such as terrain and weather. In the case of Frankstown, it was the lack of posting advanced scouts or flankers that contributed to the success of the ambush.
* To all the young that are and ever shall be: Combat is real. It is personal. Glory is not combat. Glory follows from a distance in time and/or from a different level, if it follows at all.

As a case study, the ambush at Frankstown represents frontier warfare in the American Revolution. Frankstown reinforces lessons on cultural diversity, represented by the Iroquois and challenges us to create reality: human beings and not shibboleths and stereotypes ranging from the "noble savage" to the barbarian. Human traits and universal values transcend cultures. Learning this leads to understanding. Ignoring this leads to atrophy - in societies as well as individuals. Atrophy inevitably leads to decay and death. History and philosophy teach us this.

Footnotes: Section 1

1. B. Graymont, *The Iroquois in the American Revolution*, 223.
2. H.C. Mathews, *The Mark of Honour*, 64.
3. Mathews, 82.
4. Mathews, 100.
5. E. Cruikshank, *Butler's Rangers*, 78.
6. (1) Mathews, 82
   (2) Cruikshank, 78.
7. A. Eckert, *A Sorrow in our Hearts*, 867. Eckert believes the British garrisons suffered a severe outbreak of scurvy, not the Indians as reported in the newspapers at the time.
8. Cruikshank, 78.
9. Eckert, 867.
10. Mathews, 76-77.
11. Graymont, 206. The number listed are those fit for duty. The total force was over 5100, including commissioned officers. These figures included General James Clinton's force from New York, joining even with Sullivan at Tioga on August 22nd.
12. T.S. Montgomery, ed., *Frontier Forts of Pennsylvania*, Vol. 1, 457.
13. (1) Graymont, 212; (2) Mathews, 66.
    Mathews states that even with these results (at a loss of fewer than 40 men [Graymont, 218]), Sullivan failed to capture Fort Niagara, his major objective, before the onset of winter. She intimates that Sullivan delayed too long at Wyoming, PA, which cost him valuable summer and fall campaigning time. He left Wyoming, July 31st, after numerous logistical delays, arriving at Tioga Point August 11th. However, Fort Niagara was never his objective. His orders from Washington regarding Niagara were discretionary. If Fort Niagara were his objective, he would have had a siege cannon along, which he did not. (J.R. Fisher, *A Well Executed Failure*, 47-48; 77.) Sullivan was astounded at the level of sophistication of the Iroquois, as he related in his official report to the Continental Congress. The Mohawks lived in better comforts than the white settlers, their neighbors, along the Mohawk River, having considerable numbers of livestock, vegetables, barns, houses, wagons, and farm implements.

Many of the Mohawk houses had window glass (Graymont, 147).

These figures do not include the expedition of Colonel Daniel Brodhead, who marched from Fort Pitt August 11, 1779 and returned September 14, 1979. Brodhead reported the destruction of several Delaware and Seneca towns and 500 acres of corn and vegetables (1. Graymont, 218-219. Graymont inadvertently lists September 11th for August 11th. 2."Col. Daniel Brodhead to General George Washington, September 16, 1779" and "Col. Daniel Brodhead to Gen. John Sullivan, Oct. 10, 1779", *Brodhead's Letter Book*, PA Archives, First Series, Vol. 12, 155-156 and 165-166.)

Several historical inaccuracies and inconsistencies exist concerning the Brodhead expedition, including the northern-most point of penetration into Iroquoia, route of return to Fort Pitt, and numbers and sites of Indian villages destroyed. Brodhead never got as far north as the present New York state border. The northern-most point was the village of Yoghroonwago (the name given by Brodhead or Yoroonwago, as Donehoo spells it [Donehoo, *Indian Villages and Place Names in Pennsylvania*, 263-264]) ; or Dionosadage (the correct name, according to Donehoo, 74-75), one of Cornplanter's two villages. The site was the early 20th century town of Corydon, in Warren County, PA, (Donehoo, 263) now under the waters of the Kinzua Dam.

Cornplanter was buried here. When the dam was about to be built, his remains were exhumed and reinterred on a bluff of a hill, overlooking the site of his village. The author has visited this new grave. Standing here, he found it ironic that our civilization would honor him by preserving his remains; but bury him overlooking his permanently submerged home - an eternal left-handed compliment, if ever there was one.

Brodhead, in his report to Sullivan cited above, stated that he turned back for want of shoes for his men. The author also believes that another reason was the impending expiration of enlistments for many of his non-commissioned officers and privates in the Pennsylvania 8th Regiment. ("Col. Daniel Brodhead to Col. David Shepherd", transcript 1SS175, Draper MSS in: Kellogg, L.P. *Frontier Retreat on the Upper Ohio, 1779-1781*, 98.) Brodhead had only 605 men total, including militia, (cited in his report to Washington, above). Given these numbers, perhaps a third reason was simply this: don't push your luck.

Many local historians (for example, see Wallace, *Indian Trails in Pennsylvania*, 176) believe that Brodhead returned from Venango (Franklin, PA) generally the way he began: from Mahoning (at the mouth of Mahoning Creek), after leaving the Allegheny River, to Goshgushing, the site of a Munsee (Wolf clan of the Lenni Lenape-Delaware) village at the mouth of Tionesta Creek (Donehoo, 66).

However, Brodhead stated in his letter to Washington (cited above): "The army returned via the Old Venango Road." This was a former Indian trail, part of which became an old French military/supply road from Presque Isle (Erie, PA) to the forks of the Ohio (site of Forts Dusquesne [French] and Pitt [British, then Patriot]). It ran directly north and south between Fort Pitt and Venango (Wallace, 170-173).

Besides Brodhead's direct statement, this author feels that Brodhead would have taken this route for these reasons:
* It was shorter than marching southeast from Venango to Kittanning (Kittanning, PA) and then southwest to Fort Pitt.
* His men were lacking footwear - at least the shoes were wearing thin. Brodhead stated in his report to Washington that his men's clothing was "in tatters".
* His men were carrying an additional $30,000 worth of plunder excluding their supplies, equipment and arms.
* His men were returning to their home base from a military expedition. Why prolong the march?
* Supplies were running low. They left with cattle for food but had none upon return. ("Recollections of Daniel Higgins", transcript 3S128-29, Draper MSS, in: Kellogg, 59-60.)

Kellogg has cited several primary documents from Brodhead's expeditions, including not only his letters to Washington and Sullivan, but also from his men and Indian enemies. These were interviewed by Lyman Copeland Draper (compiler of the Draper Manuscripts) after the Revolution. In regards to the Brodhead expedition, Native Americans interviewed include Charles O'Bail (Cornplanter's son), Blacksnake (a Seneca warrior at the time of the battle), and Captain John Decker (Dah-gan-non-do: "He who patches"), a Seneca (Kellogg, 62-66).

"The Recollections of Capt. Matthew Jack" (one of Brodhead's captains) is interesting in that he, along with Samuel Brady (Captain of Brady's Rangers - see Section 7), took two companies of men and marched northwest from Venango up French Creek, where they destroyed a Native American village called Mahusquechikokow. This village was either at or below present day Meadville, PA. ("Recollections of Capt. Matthew Jack. transcript 6NN188, Draper MSS, in Kellogg, 61.)

Another member of Brodhead's force corroborates Brodhead's statement and the author's above premise regarding the route back: "...after crossing French Creek at its mouth, took over the hills direct to Pittsburgh" (Recollections of Daniel Higgins," cited above).

The above sources and others cited by Kellogg, heretofore unknown or forgotten by historians, give details of the expedition as well as the only skirmish fought. This occured two or three miles below the mouth of present Brokenstraw Creek, on the Allegheny. Both the Patriot and Native American views on this skirmish are presented by Kellogg.

14. Mathews, 81.
15. Mathews, 83
16. Mathews, 86.
17. Mathews, 66-68.
18. Eckert, 150.

Footnotes: Section 2

1. U.J. Jones, *History of the Early Settlement at the Juniata Valley*, 298.
2. Paul A.W. Wallace, *Indian Paths of Pennsylvania*, 51.
3. G.P. Donehoo, *Indian Villages and Place Names in Pennsylvania*, 8.
4. Jones, 302.
5. Donehoo, 61-62.
6. (1) Donehoo, 68. (2) Wallace, 51.
7. Donehoo, 68.
8. Wallace, 51.
9. Pennsylvania Archives, First Series, Vol. 6, "Col. John Piper to Council, 1778", in: J.B. Whisker, *Bedford County (Pennsylvania) in the American Revolution*, 25.
10. Eugene R. Craine, *The Story of Fort Roberdeau*, 3.

Footnotes: Section 3

1. Carl Waldman, "Algonquian", *Encyclopedia of Native American Tribes*, p. 12. Note: for Algonquian, see also footnote 8, Section 4.
2. (1) Hazel C. Mathews, *The Mark of Honour*, 18-19; (2) Sherrill Whiton, "The American Periods," *Elements of Interior Design & Decoration*, 286-289.
3. Mathews, 19.
4. Mathews, 25-26
5. Mathews, 25-26.
6. Mathews, 21.
7. Mathews, 22.
8. Mathews, 23.
9. Mathews, 20.
10. Mathews, 24.
11. Mathews, 24.
12. Mathews, 24.
13. PA Archives, First Series, Vol. 6, "Col. John Piper to Council, 1778, " in: James Whisker, *Bedford County in the American Revolution*, 25
14. (1) Thomas Lynch Montgomery, *Frontier Forts of PA*, Vol. I, p. 495; (2) J. Simpson Africa, *History of Huntingdon and Blair Counties, Pennsylvania*, 194-195.
15. Montgomery, 492.
16. Montgomery, 492.
17. U.J. Jones, *History of the Early Settlement of the Juniata Valley*, 303.
18. Montgomery, 492.
19. R. Emerson, *Fort Roberdeau: The Garrison and Military Life, 1778-1780*, 6-7.
20. Montgomery, 497.
21. Montgomery, 497.
22. Montgomery, 497.
23. R. Emerson, "Debacle on the Juniata: the Battle of Frankstown, 1781", *The Mansion*, 1. Emerson believes that this blockhouse was distinct from Fort Fetter, though at times in local histories it was called Fort Fetter. It was built after the original Fort Fetter and was in existence

by June, 1781. Emerson bases his conclusions upon analysis of primary sources, including pension declarations of two Revolutionary War soldiers. These two men served tours of duty at different times, yet both were engaged in building a fort in the same geographic area. Emerson has reviewed his findings, sources and his analysis with the author, who concurs. (For locations of the Frankstown Blockhouse and Fort Fetter, refer to Section 10, Figures 10.1. and 10.2.)

Footnotes: Section 4

1. Paul A.W. Wallace, *Indians of Pennsylvania*, 89.
2. Peter P. Pratt, "A Perspective on Oneida Archaeology", in: Funk, R.E. and Hayes III, C.F., eds. *Current Perspectives in Northeast Archaeology: Essays in Honor of William A. Ritchie*, 64.
3. Barbara Graymont, *The Iroquois in the American Revolution*, 6.
4. (1) Wallace, 86; (2) James A. Tuck, "The Iroquois Confederacy" in: Reprints from Scientific American: *New World Archaeology, Theoretical and Cultural Transformations*, 200.
5. Wallace, 110.
6. Wallace, 57.
7. Graymont, 24.
8. Algonquian was one major language grouping of Northeast Native American nations. Iroquoian was the other.
9. For the reader to better understand Iroquoian and French relationships - or the lack thereof - he is referred to the 7 volume series, *France and England in North America*, by the 19th century historian, Francis Parkman.
10. Tuck, 199-200.
11. Isabel Thompson Kelsay, *Joseph Brant: 1743-1807: Man of Two Worlds*, 2-3.
12. Hazel C. Mathews, *The Mark of Honour*, map, facing p. 52.
13. Wallace, 86.
14. Wallace, 87.
15. Graymont, 16.
16. Dr. George P. Donehoo, *A History of the Indian Villages and Place Names in Pennsylvania*, 99-100; 154.
17. (1) Donehoo, 154; (2) Kelsay, 127; (3) Mathews, 27; (4) Graymont, map facing 1.
18. Mathews, 27-28; 77-79.
19. Tuck, 198.
20. Pratt, 57.
21. Graymont, 9.
22. Delores Elliott, "Otsiningo, an Example of an Eighteenth Century Settlement Pattern", in: Robert R. Funk, and Charles F. Hayes III,

       ed., *Current Perspectives in Northeastern Archaeology: Essays in Honor of William A. Ritchie*, 96-97.
23.   Francis W. Halsey, *The Old New York Frontier*, 226.
24.   (1) Tuck, 190-200; (2) Pratt, 51-69.
25.   Gregory Evans Dowd, *A Spirited Resistance: The North American Indian Struggle for Unity, 1745-1815,* 3.
For Native American peoples, power was focal to all levels of existence. At the physical level, power meant life: to eat, to attract a lover, to defeat enemies, to slay animals, to influence other people. On the spiritual level, power meant the ability to visit with God, to communicate with animals, to heal. Some things possessed more power than others. To gain the favor of those entities, from whatever world, having power, the Native Americans practiced rituals and held ceremonies. To neglect ritual was to lose power. (Dowd, 1-4.)

Among rituals were the rights of war. It was, for example, "bad" to mix powers: the warrior man, in his "war mode", with a female (captive, lover or wife) in her "life mode": the power to give life, to birth. (Dowd, 9.) Hence it is rare to read historical accounts of Native American warriors raping captives taken in a raid. It is certainly permissible to display power over one's enemy by torturing and scalping while in one's "war mode", but one could not mix the two powers. Should a warrior of any other culture or race remain stoic and sing his death song while being tortured, he had power over you, the torturer. This signified that his clan, relatives, tribe would do likewise to the torturer: "What ye sow, so shall ye reap". Hence the importance of rituals in preparing for war by dance: ritual was the bridge for transferring from a "peace mode" power to a "war mode" power. And the same upon return to the village: the warrior in his "war mode" *had* to transfer back to his "peace mode". Again, this was done by ritual. The author surmises that running the gauntlet was a "cleansing" ritual, "cleansing" the captive of power impurities as well as reinforcing the power of the village and its warriors over the captive.

Dowd (see Bibliography) researches the Delaware, Shawnee, Cherokee, and Creek, and cites copious primary sources who were observers of these 18th century Native peoples' practices. Little is given in Dowd's material on the Iroquois, per se. However, the author surmises that their traditions were also believed and practiced in Iroquoia. (For example, see the concept of power inextricably related to the "mourning war" in footnote 37.)

It is interesting to note further that Dowd's work, cited in this footnote, concerns itself primarily with religious revival among the aforementioned Native peoples at the end of the 18th and beginning of the 19th centuries. The peoples were to throw off the tradition of the European culture which was contaminating their power. Only by being "pure" - adhering to the rituals and customs and/or developing new ones which reestablished contact with the power sources - could the people survive and prosper. Cultural change produced backlash: for every action, there is an equal and opposite reaction. Human nature does not change - only technology. At the end of the 20th century, the United States, faced with disintegration of its society, its standard of living, has seen a religious revival of the "right" as manifested in the national political elections of 1994.

26. Graymont, 13.
27. Graymont, 13. For example, the father of Shikellamy, vice consul at Shamokin (Sunbury, PA) for the Iroquois, was French; his mother, Cayuga. When two years old, he was taken captive by the Oneidas and raised by them. Even as a captive and adopted by this member nation, since his mother was Cayuga, he took his nationality from her. (Wallace, *Indians in Pennsylvania*, 178.)
28. Graymont, 13.
29. Graymont, 21.
30. Kelsay, 32.
31. Kelsay, 188.
32. Graymont, 123.
33. Kelsay, 102.
34. Kelsay, 49, 79, 97 (footnote 4: 669).
35. The Wyoming Massacre is a classic public relations propaganda coup,

and is still perpetuated to this day by local historians. Many of Colonel Zebulon Butler's militia were killed in battle: 227 scalps were taken according to British reports. Colonel Dennison of the patriot militia reported that 301 men had been killed in battle. He did not mention *any* massacre taking place. Primary sources place Joseph Brant on the New York Frontier on July 3rd, the day of the battle, and afterward. One of the Seneca War Chiefs (see above), Sayenqueragtha, was in command of the Indians during all of the Wyoming campaign. (See Bibliography, Graymont, 168-174; Kelsay, 218-222.) Neither was there any such massacre at "Queen Esther's Rock" (involving Esther Montour and/or Catherine Montour). Though women did accompany expeditions, *none* were present on this particular expedition (Graymont: 174).

36. (1) Kelsay, 190-193; (2) Mary Beacock Fryer, *King's Men: the Soldier Founders of Ontario*, 32.

37. Kelsay, 21. Richter (see Bibliography) gives a scholarly account of the importance of the "mourning war" to Iroquoian culture, and how this impacted war tactics. For example, the Iroquois attempted to minimize loss, believing that violent deaths of their warriors caused them to be excluded from the villages of the dead and their spirits were doomed to spend eternity roving, seeking revenge. Those so killed were even buried away from the others in their village cemeteries in case their angry spirits disturbed those resting in peace. (D.K. Richter, "War and Culture: The Iroquois Experience", 535-536.)

No wonder, then, that the Iroquois engaged in tactics such as hit-and-run raids that would minimize loss - especially in the face of modern European and Euro-American arms.

For Richter, the "mourning war" served three functions in Iroquoian society: (Richter, 529-537)

* Restoration of lost population (see below).
* Dealing with death in their ranks on a societal level. When a person died, the power (see footnote 25) of his nation, village, clan, and

relatives was diminished. To compensate, ceremonies had to be conducted (probably as soon as possible) to transfer the deceased's name, social duties and roles to a successor. (Perhaps this is why the warriors gave up attainment of subsequent military objectives in his raids - see text.)

* Dealing with death in their ranks on a personal level. Rituals and ceremonies channeled emotions. A socially sanctioned channel was a war raid to see captives to alleviate both personal pain and help restore a sense of collective power to the nation, village, clan and/or relatives.

For the author, the "mourning war" additionally served the functions of training a boy in warfare as well as training in such tactics of captives of all races adopted into the village. The Iroquois were proficient warriors. They had to learn to fight together.

The League, incidentally, ultimately envisioned a "League of Peace", a day in which their League of Peace extended to all peoples. There was an alternative to the "mourning war". This was represented by council deliberations and diplomacy. [Richter, 536.]

However, European contact intensified the purposes of the "mourning war". Contact lead to acquisition of European diseases, for which the Iroquois and other Native American peoples had no immunity. Richter estimates that by the 1640's, the Iroquois had lost one half of their entire population to disease. [537] This necessitated replenishment of the population.

Firearms added greatly to the probability that every war party would suffer casualties. Firearms took longer to load than the bow and arrow; their roar signaled presence. Surprise became more difficult.

38. Kelsay, 21-22. Both sides, patriot rebel and British loyalist, and their Indian allies, took scalps. The state of Pennsylvania offered official bounties. $1500.00 for each male prisoner and $1000.00 for each scalp. ([1] Fryer, 160; [2] PA Colonial Records, Vol. 12, "Minutes of

the Supreme Executive Council", 311.) Col. Daniel Brodhead, commander of the Western District of Fort Pitt, was so afraid of his Delaware Indian allies operating as scouts and with his rangers and Christian Delawares (who sent him information) being killed, that he wrote to the Pennsylvania Supreme Executive Council and urged that they rescind the bounty offer. ([1] PA Archives, First Series, Vol. 7, 569-572: "President Reed to Col. Brodhead, 1779; [2] PA Archives, First Series, Vol. 7, 524-526: "John Hackenwelder to Col. Brodhead, 1779, Coochocking, June 30th, 1779"; [3] PA Archives, First Series, Vol. 12, 284, "Daniel Brodhead's Letter Book: No. 160, To Col. John Evans, 1780, Head Q'rs Fort Pitt, May 20th, 1780".

39. (1) Graymont, 37-39; (2) Kelsay, 179-180.
40. Kelsay, 255.
41. Kelsay, 212.
42. As part of the General John Burgoyne campaign, Burgoyne, moving south from Canada and down Lake George (New York state), was expected to link with General William Howe, expected to move north from New York City. It was the linkage of these two armies that was anticipated to cut the rebel colonies off, isolating the New England colonies from New York. Howe never moved out of New York. Burgoyne was defeated at Saratoga (Freeman's Farm: September 19, 1777; Bemis Heights: October 7, 1777) and the surrender of his army precipitated France to formally ally itself with the American colonies.

In the meantime, British provincial troops (including rangers - See Section 5) and their Indian allies, under the command of Lieutenant Colonel Barry St. Leger, were to give Burgoyne support on his right flank and eventually link up with Burgoyne. Such support would be the investment and capitulation of the former Fort Stanwix (called Fort Schuyler by the patriots - at the site of Rome, NY), then move down the Mohawk River Valley. St. Leger did lay siege to the fort, but due to his not bringing heavy siege guns in the campaign (which the Iroquois and Daniel Claus told him were needed), the siege was broken - by Benedict Arnold.

During the siege was fought the battle of Oriskany, a pyrrhic victory for the British. The Tryon County, New York, militia, under Major General Nicholas Herkimer, was almost exterminated; Herkimer himself died soon after of his wounds, after his leg was amputated. The Seneca lost five important war chiefs (though not their two hereditary war chiefs); collective Iroquois losses were 33 killed and 29 wounded (Graymont, 138). The real impact of Oriskany is that it drew the Iroquois into the Revolutionary War on the side of the British.

43. Kelsay, 199, footnote 39.
44. Graymont, 71-72.
45. (1) Graymont, 50-51; 328; (2) Fryer, 26-30.
46. Fryer, 28.
47. Fryer, 136.
48. Fryer, 135. Guy Johnson was Sir William Johnson's nephew and son-in-law. Upon Sir William's death in 1774, Guy Johnson was appointed Superintendent of Indian Affairs of the Indian Department, Northern District, of the 13 colonies. Daniel Claus was Superintendent of Canadian Indians only. The Colonial Secretary, Lord George Germain, did not respect Guy Johnson. In his correspondence, Claus raved about Joseph Brant: he could do no wrong. Claus continuously chastised Butler, who could do no right. Guy Johnson also disliked Butler, for whatever reasons. Policy certainly entered into it. Johnson, in the Spring of 1776 after returning to Canada from England (accompanied by Claus and Brant, among others), was furious with Butler, according to Fryer (p. 136) for not having a host of Iroquois ransack the rebel frontiersmen's homes. Because of Butler's original orders to help keep the Iroquois neutral and Joseph Brant's urging the Iroquois to war, a coolness developed between Brant and Butler that perhaps was never quite overcome, though they had to work with one another. Careful reading of Fryer, Graymont, and Kelsay (see Bibliography) reveals the conflicts among the British allies.

Regarding the actions of Butler, Graymont (Chapter 4, especially pp. 97-98) gives evidence that Butler was attempting to get the Iroquois to break their neutrality since his appointment to Niagara. Fryer and Kelsay state that his actions changed as his instructions changed (see Kelsay 186-187 compared to 196, for example). It is interesting to compare Graymont (97-98) with Fryer (135). Given a review of the evidence to date, this author agrees with Fryer and Kelsay to the effect that Butler's actions changed with his instructions and orders.

49. Graymont, 125-128.
50. Graymont, 83; 94; 136; 138.
51. Kelsay, 25-37.
52. Wallace, A.F.C. King of the Delawares: Teedyuscung, 1700-1763, 59-66; 238; 254-261.

This source is listed here because Wallace presents a case history example throughout this book of what Kelsay is stating: the bribing and cajoling of individual Native Americans by alcohol in order to get them drunk and sign deeds. In this case, presented in these pages by Wallace, it is Connecticut's Susquehanna Land Company's activities to "purchase" the Wyoming Valley (including the present sites of Scranton and Wilkes Barre, PA) from the Six Nations. Wallace also strongly suggests the murder of Teedyuscung, a Delaware (Lenni Lanape) was instigated by this company after he protested and refused to leave the valley.

Footnotes: Section 5

1. Mary Beacock Fryer, *King's Men: the Soldier Founders of Ontario*, 138.
2. Hazel C. Mathews, *The Mark of Honour*, 71.
3. John H. Carter, "Indian Incursions in Old Northumberland County During the Revolutionary War: 1777-1782 in: C.F. Snyder, ed., *Northumberland County in the American Revolution*, 373-376.
4. Fryer, 135.
5. Fryer, 14, 17, 137-138. A "beating order" implied, in British military tradition, for the recruiter to travel the country with a drummer. This method proved impossible to carry out literally in the rebellious colonies; recruiters needed to move about in rebellious country in secret. However, the term was still used; and a recruiter with a drummer could function together in Canada.
6. Kelsay, *Joseph Brant: 1743-1807, Man of Two Worlds*, 120.
7. Fryer, 135.
8. Fryer, 137.
9. Fryer, 133. A portrait of him, the only one the author has seen, is included in Fryer's work.
10. Fryer, 133. If any of these descriptions were made by Claus, the reader will recall from Section 4 that for Daniel Claus, Butler could do no right; Joseph Brant, no wrong. Nor did Guy Johnson have any real love for the father. Perhaps Guy himself felt very insecure after acquiring Sir William Johnson's position. Sir William was truly a "legend in his own time" and enjoyed the respect of the Iroquois. Guy had large moccasins to fill. Claus and Guy Johnson were not respected by their supervisors. Regardless of the truth about John Butler's traits, the comments of Governor Haldimand regarding Walter Butler seem valid for this author. Walter did not have the Indian's respect nor could he control them at the Cherry Valley Massacre (New York) in the winter of 1778. Daniel Claus did enjoy the respect of diverse tribes of Canadian Indians. It was they who also got his job restored after he was replaced (Graymont, 125).

11. Fryer, 143. John Butler turned over his field command to Captain William Caldwell, his acting senior captain. Walter Butler was himself in ill health and recuperating at Niagara and not yet in his father's ranger corps (Fryer, 144).
12. Mathews, 161.
13. Kelsay, 222.
14. Mathews, 67-68; 140.
15. (1) John Richard Alden, *The American Revolution*, 60; 66-67; (2) Major James R. Williamson, "Tories Along the Susquehanna", 61.
16. Fryer, 12; 16.
17. Alden, 88.
18. (1) PA Archives, First Series, Vol. 12., "Col. Brodhead's Letter Book", 203; 274; (2) PA Archives, First Series, Vol. 6, "Examination of Richard Weston, 1778", 542-538; (3) Williamson, 65-66; (4) L. Fossler, "Samuel Wallis: Colonial Merchant, Secret Agent", 108-115. (5) J. Bakeless, *Turncoats, Traitors and Heroes*, 294-301. The prominent merchant, landowner, and captain in Northumberland County militia, Samuel Wallis, allowed the bastioned Fort Muncy to be built only several hundred yards from his stone house above the present Muncy, PA. He was Benedict Arnold's courier to Major John Andre. His estate was code-named "Peter" by Andre (Bakeless, 294). Andre and Arnold (West Point Commander) conspired to give up West Point to the British. These activities commenced in 1779, with Arnold's marriage to the Philadelphia belle, Peggy Shippen (Alden, 209-210). Wallis was under military contract by the Continental Congress to produce campaign maps for the Sullivan expedition (Section 1). He produced bogus maps. Wallis was never caught or suspected. His activities did not become known until the 20th century.
19. (1) Cruikshank, *Butler's Rangers*, 44; (2) Mathews, 31-41.
20. Graymont, *The Iroquois in the American Revolution*, 167-168.
21. Cruikshank, 44.
22. (1) Williamson, 61-64; (2) Mathews, 31-41.
23. Alden, 87.
24. R.G. Swartz, "Ranger Companies of the Pennsylvania Frontier and Northumberland County During the American Revolution," 249-250.
25. R.G. Swartz, "Fort Muncy During the American Revolution," *Now*

          and Then Magazine, August 1994, 28-46.
26. (1) Frederick A. Godcharles, "The Battle of Fort Freeland" in Charles F. Snyder, ed., *Northumberland County in the American Revolution*, 143 (2) R.G. Swartz, "Roles and Analysis of the Fort Freeland Relief Force: July 28, 1779" a research paper submitted to Warrior Run-Fort Freeland Heritage Society, Dec. 9, 1994.
27. Jon Baughman, *Philip's Rangers,* 12-16.
28. Fryer, 158.
29. T. L. Montgomery, ed. *Report of the Commission to Create the Site of the Frontier Forts of Pennsylvania,* Vol. 2, 290-323.
30. Kelsay, 312-313. This was almost totally an Indian victory. Butler's Rangers were coming in support at the time the battle was fought. A few whites fought with Brant, including George Girty, brother of Simon Girty, Pennsylvania patriot turned loyalist and scout employed by the British from Fort Detroit.
31. Fryer, 163, 167. Swartz contends, given the research, that approximately 20% of his full corps consisted of Pennsylvanians.
32. Fryer, 137.
33. Fryer, 137.
34. Fryer, 15.
35. Fryer, 138.
36. Fryer, 138.
37. Fryer, 137-138.
38. Fryer, 146-147.
39. Joseph Doddridge, *Notes on the Settlement and Indian Wars,* 91-92,
40. Fryer, 146-147. The author cannot substantiate these facts regarding Butler's Rangers uniforms. Fryer lists no sources for such facts.
41. Fryer, 147.
42. Fryer, 147.
43. Fryer, 147.
44. Richard B. LaCrosse, Jr., *The Frontier Rifleman,* 14. At the time of this writing, Swartz is trying to gain a consistent time of 1 1/2 minutes. The Pennsylvania ranger and captain, Sam Brady, could - like Daniel Boone, Simon Kenton and a few others - allegedly fire and reload on the run (Eckert, *A Sorrow in Our Heart,* 852-853). A Lancaster, PA, gunsmith has told Swartz that 150 things can go wrong

when loading and firing a long rifle; and that they will go wrong when firing at a deer (or a man). Thus such skills on the run are further remarkable. Loading it in approximately 30 seconds is no small feat, either, involving at least six major steps: (1) pouring the correct amount of powder down a small muzzle hole from a measure via a powder horn; (2) placing a patch and proper size ball on the muzzle hole; (3) ramming the patch and ball down the length of the barrel (this could be using a starter ramrod, then the regular); (4) removing the ramrod; (5) placing special priming powder from another flask or horn into the flash pan that creates the spark through the touch hole to ignite the powder to propel the ball out the barrel; (6) cocking, aiming, and firing. Hence expressions that are fading from usage: "straight as a ramrod"; "(He's/She's) a flash in the pan".

45. Charles R. Casada, "18th Century Camoflage", 48.
46. Fryer, 138. Fryer has three phases; Swartz includes fighting Sullivan in New York as a phase unto itself. This involved the skirmish at Chemung, August 13, 1779; the pitched battle of Newtown, August 29, 1779; and the ambush at the swamp at the head of Lake Conesus, September 13, 1779. Butler's lost heavily at Newtown and won at the two ambushes. Butler and Brant did not want to offer battle at Newtown; the warriors and other chiefs made the decision to fight. The Chemung ambush took place between present day Waverly, PA, and Elmira, NY; the Battle of Newtown occurred near present day Elmira, NY. On the day of the battle, three Ranger officers and several men in the ranks were suffering from ague (Graymont, 209). The Lake Conesus ambush site is southwest of present day Geneseo, NY. In these three engagements, estimated casualties (killed, wounded, missing) include:

    Butler's Indian allies: 24
    Butler's Rangers   8
    Sullivan's troops: 92
    Sullivan's Indian allies: 2

(These figures exclude Brodhead's concomitant Western expedition up the Allegheny River. These numbers are culled from Fryer, 152-153; Graymont, 204, 212, and 217. There are discrepancies, as there are from opposing sides in any war.)

47. Donehoo, *Indian Villages and Place Names in Pennsylvania*, 108. "Mingo" was the term applied to all Iroquois, regardless of tribe or clan, living in the Ohio River drainage area. It was an Algonquian (a collective linguistic group of NE United States Indian tribes; the other major group was Iroquoian) term meaning "stealthy" or "treacherous". The whites had the same connotation when they used this term.

48. (1) Donehoo, 129; (2) Major Robert Rogers, *Journals of Major Robert Rogers*, particularly 59-70. The serious student of the Revolutionary War on the frontiers cannot understand it without studying Roger's tactics. Today, we would call these "guerrilla warfare" or "counter-insurgency" tactics.

49. Mathews, 60-61.

50. In Pennsylvania, the image of the birch bark canoe is a myth. It was not endemic to Pennsylvania, nor to the Ohio River country. Elm was indigenous to both areas. In the Ohio River country, Shawnee warriors could build an elm bark canoe in about two hours. Birch was not indigenous to Ohio. Elm was flexible; it would not rot. Hence, upon crossing a river, it was sunk, with rocks and water in it. This would hide it so it could be used upon return. (Eckert, 864-865). However, if used on portage, the elm bark canoe was dead weight; when used in water, it was awkward. Other Pennsylvania woods, such as poplar, sycamore, walnut and tulip were heavy and clumsy to use. (Paul A.W. Wallace, *Indian Paths of Pennsylvania*, 2)

51. Dale Van Every, *A Company of Heroes*, 77. Cold and wet weather combined with the type of footwear described in the narrative also greatly contributed to frontiersmen suffering from rheumatism. Hence, the men slept with their feet to the fire to help prevent or cure it, as much as possible (Doddridge, 92).

52. (1) Mathews, 69; (2) Fryer, 163, 166, 159, 162; (3) Cruikshank, 76.

53. Fryer, 161.

Footnotes: Section 6

1. "The Military System of Pennsylvania During the Revolutionary War", *Information Leaflet #3*, Pennsylvania Historic and Museum Commission, 2.
2. "The Military System of Pennsylvania....", 2.
3. Arthur J. Alexander, "Pennsylvania's Revolutionary Militia", 18-19.
4. Alexander, 20.
5. William P. Clarke, Chapter II: "Laws of the Revolutionary Period, 1775-1883", in *Official History of the Militia and National Guard*, 17. The PA Colonial Records and the PA Archives contain a plethora of correspondence: for example, from President Reed to Col. Hunter. Reed would be President of the Supreme Executive Council; Hunter, though a colonel, was County Lieutenant of Northumberland County.
6. Alexander, 20.
7. (1) Clarke, 19; (2) Alexander, 20, 21.
8. Alexander, 21.
9. Alexander, 21.
10. Clarke, 21.
11. Alexander, 21.
12. Clarke, 21.
13. Alexander, 21.
14. Clarke, 22.
15. Alexander, 21-22.
16. Robert L. Emerson, *Fort Roberdeau: The Garrison and Military Life, 1778-1780*, 17-19.
17. (1) Emerson, 17-19; (2) Richard Irwin Rossbacher, "Facing the Second Front: Chapter 12", in *Now Remembered: Living PA History Through 1900*, 319-324.
18. PA Archives, First Series, Vol. 6, "Thomas Smith and George Woods to Council", 39-40, in James B. Whisker, *Bedford County (Pennsylvania) in the American Revolution*, 23-24.
19. Emerson, 12.
20. The site of the old Delaware Indian village burned by the 1756 Armstrong expedition in the French and Indian War; now the site of Kittanning, PA.

21. (1) Emerson, 12-14; (2) PA Archives, First Series, Vol. 6, 542-543: "Examination of Richard Weston, 1778".
22. Emerson, 15.
23. PA Archives, First Series, Vol. 7, 434-435: "President Reed to Thomas Scott, 1779, Philadelphia, May 22, 1779".
24. Emerson, 15-16.
25. PA Archives, First Series, Vol. 7, 434-435.
26. PA Archives, First Series, Vol. 6, "Lieutenant Samuel Hunter to Council, 1778, Sunbury 26th May, 1778", 552-553. For Swartz, it is no wonder that Hunter ordered an evacuation of the entire West Branch of the Susquehanna (from Fort Reid, Lock Haven, PA, through Fort Muncy, Muncy, PA, and south) within 1 1/2 months from the date of this letter.
27. PA Archives, Second Series, Vol. 3, "Memorial of the Inhabitants of the West Branch, Muncy, June 10th, 1778", 176-178.
28. Thwaites, Reuben G. and Kellogg, Louise Phelps, *Frontier Defense on the Upper Ohio, 1777-1778*, fn. 70, 198.
29. "Report of Commissioners" (Commissioners to Edward Hand), transcript 3NN21-23, Draper MSS, in: Thwaites and Kellogg, 238-240.

Footnotes: Section 7

1. PA Archives, Third Series, Vol. 23, 194-356.
2. Charles Fisher Snyder, "The Militia of Northumberland County During the Revolution", in: Charles F. Snyder, ed., *Northumberland County in the American Revolution*, 327-355.
3. PA Archives, First Series, Vol. 7, "Lt. Saml. Hunter to Pres. Reed, 1778, Sunbury 13th December, 1778", 116-118.
4. Richard Irwin Rossbacher, "Facing the Second Front: Chapter 12", in *Now Remembered: Living Pennsylvania History Through 1900*, 324. Perhaps the political issues of Bedford County played a part in this (Section 6).
5. PA Archives, First Series, Vol. 6, "Thomas Smith and George Woods to Council, Nov. 27, 1777", 39-40.
6. PA Archives, First Series, Vol. 7, "Pres. Reed to Lieutenants, etc., 1779, Philadelphia, March 27th, 1779", 267-268. This letter was sent to the lieutenants of Bedford, Westmoreland, and Northumberland Counties.
7. "Extract from the Minutes of Congress, 25th Feb'y, 1778", in Journals of the WPA, Vol. 66, No. 3: "Pension Declarations for Revolutionary Service in Columbia County: Moses Van Campen", Library, Northumberland County Historical Society, Sunbury, PA.
8. "Extract from the Minutes of the General Assembly of Pennsylvania: March 29, 1779", in Journals of the WPA, Vol. 66, No. 3: "Pension Declarations for Revolutionary Service in Columbia County: Moses Van Campen", Library, Northumberland County Historical Society, Sunbury, PA.
9. Regarding Sam Brady, the source is : J.F. Meginness, *Otzinachson: A History of the West Branch Valley of the Susquehanna*, p. 599. Other sources for these statements include *Northumberland County in the American Revolution*.

It is possible this ambush of Boone's on was the only time that a large force of Butler's men were really caught off guard. (McDonell to Butler, Tioga Pointe, Aug. 5th, 1779, Haldimand

Papers, National Archives of Canada, MG 21, Add. Mss. 21760, [B-100], 223-225 [on reel H-1446].)

Boone, not knowing the fort had already capitulated, advanced into open ground and was heading to the fort when he saw the smoke arising from it. (Meginness, 597) They made a fight of it, attempting to retreat into the thickets from whence they came.

The pond, bogs, are quiet now. Here in late summer, you can hear the katydids; grasses stir slightly in a languid breeze. Allow yourself to drift and you can hear the warrior's squaws as they gather up the white's possessions. See them riding sidesaddle as they mimic the white woman. Allow yourself to drift and you can smell the sulphur, smell and see the smoke of guns drift and settle slowly over the grass. Hear now the peculiar sound of the tomahawk smashing through the heads of Boone's men as they lay wounded, helpless, crying for mercy. Ironic, isn't it? This stream, even before the battle, was called Warrior Run. Boone's and Kemplins's men, too, were warriors.

Mary Jemison (James E. Seaver, *Life of Mary Jemison,* 186-187) stated that her Iroquois husband, Hiokatoo (a subchief at this battle) was scalping wounded rebels prior to Boone's attack; and that one of Boone's men continued to shoot in sequence three Indians holding a flag - sequence: each holding the flag held by the prior warrior. The flag in question was either the fort's flag or the flag of capitulation. This so incensed Hiokatoo that he then attacked Boone's party. Swartz has found this reason not collaborating with other primary sources of those present: Swartz feels that the slaying was of Boone's men, primarily, after the battle. The battle for the fort itself, earlier that morning, took five patriot lives.

The overall leader of the Indians was Cornplanter, one of the two hereditary Iroquois war chiefs (Graymont, *Iroquois in the American Revolution,* 262). Local historians have always claimed that Hiokatoo commanded the Indians. Captain John McDonell commanded Butler's Rangers. (American sources list McDonald. This is in error.) He was well liked by them. (Fryer, *King's Men*, 149. On this page, Fryer confuses McDonald [Major Donald McDonald, Royal Highland Emigrants - another provincial corps] with McDonell as well.) They were accompanied by some British army regulars (8th Regiment of Foot.)

The patriot forces coming to the fort's rescue and who ambushed McDonell and Cornplanter, were led by Captain Hawkins Boone, overall comander (killed), Captains John and Samuel Dougherty (militia), Captain Thomas Kemplin, Kemplin's Rangers. (In local sources, Kemplin is spelled diverse ways. Hence he is lost from history and his rangers from this battle. This author's spelling is in accordance with the spelling given by his widow in her pension declaration of 1788 [source: Pension for Revolutionary Service: Northumberland County, Journals of the WPA, Vol. 61, No. 2, Library, Northumberland County Historical Society, Sunbury, PA]). John's younger brother, Samuel, was killed in this battle. On the way, Samuel warned John that they were going to be defeated and not to take part in it. John replied that if he were afraid, go back. Sam's response was, to the effect: "A Daugherty is not a coward, and I'll fight as bravely as you'll fight." (On Daugherty, see Meginness, *Otzinachson*, 600.) John was taken prisoner to Canada. Kemplin survived, but was killed with his son while on duty in 1781.

Boone should have known -perhaps he did know- that the fort had surrendered, for one of Boone's advance scouts, a McMahon, accidently stumbled into the then prisoners-of-war who told him they were prisoners. Hawkins Boone's wife, Jane, in 1839 stated such: that he implored his men to follow him to save the women and children. (Jane Fortnebaugh's Declaration: in John C. Carter, "New Light on the Battle of Fort Freeland", in Charles F. Snyder, ed., *Northumberland County in the American Revolution,* 161. Jane was with her husband that day, July 27th, at Fort Boone.) McMahon barely escaped with his life while bullets hit all around him as he was running back to Boone's fort, built by Hawkins Boone. Boone was caught in the open after leaving his chosen site of ambush, opposite the victorious raiding party on Warrior Run, but perhaps not in his attempt, as some have said, to reach Fort Freeland. When the British and Indians got around his rear and stationed themselves in an old grist mill, Boone tried to fight his way out and tried to gain open ground toward Fort Montgomery. (Meginness, 598.)

The sad, ironic tragedy of this battle was that the women and children were already saved. McDonell, as apparent over-all commander (for he signed the articles of capitulation), allowed the women, children, and old men to leave, in an orderly manner, for Sunbury. Surviving male defenders of Fort Freeland were made prisoners. Mrs. Kirk, a woman in Fort Freeland, dressed her son, William, described as effeminate in appearance, in women's clothing; he escaped with the women.

Another sad tragedy is that both forts, Freeland and Boone, had ample warning from scouts of a large force "heading down". Other forts on the West Branch were abandoned. The garrisons of Freeland (commanded by John Lytle, Northumberland militia) and Boone decided to remain. Freeland was now the northern-most fort remaining occupied. All garrisoned troops of the Continental Army stationed in the West Branch had been ordered to join Sullivan's forces, assembling up the North Branch of the Susquehanna.

In their patriotic zeal, some writers claimed that Boone's ambush caused immediately 30 British and Indian casualties (cited by F.A. Godcharles, "The Battle of Fort Freeland", in: Charles F. Snyder, ed. *Northumberland County in the American Revolution,* 138.) One source claimed 150 (Meginness, fn, p. 602). Godcharles, 138, cites a then present-day source, one John Buyers, who writes that the enemy lost 8 or 10. (This Buyers' letter is also in PA Archives, First Series, Vol. 7, p. 592.) McDonell reported one Indian killed, another wounded. (E. Cruikshank, *Butler's Rangers,* 66.)

That Boone's men fought and probably fought well is attested to by the fact that McDonell stated he was attacked by 70 to 80 men

(Cruikshank, 66). Cruikshank also reports (66) that McDonell stated that after the capitulation, the Indians were in search of cattle (an objective to the campaign: Graymont, 202), and thus allowed the relief force to advance undetecte; surprised, the Indians took Boone in the flank. McDonell, in his report to Butler (cited above: McDonell to Butler, August 5, 1779), states that the Indians engaged this relief force in the left flank, while the rangers and regulars attacked them in the front. McDonell also states that none of this rescue party would have survived if it had not been for the thick overgrowth along Warrior Run. After all order was gone, these thickets helped hide several of Boone's men.

The author cannot ascertain from the eyewitness and primary source accounts how long the organized fight of Boone's lasted. According to Meginnes, 597, it started about 11:00 AM, about two hours after the fort capitulated. McDonell states the fort surrendered at 10:00 AM; two hours later, he was attacked (McDonell to Butler, Tioga Point, August 5, 1779, cited above).

One survivor, according to Meginness, 598, a man named Doyle (William Doyle, most likely, listed as a private in Captain Thomas Kemplin's Ranging Company muster role for June 15th, 1779) whose company served for a nine month enlistment [PA Archives, Second Series, Vol. 124, 334-335, in Charles Fisher Snyder, "The Militia of Northumberland County During the Revolution," 304-305]), darted into a thicket of hazel bushes and remained there until night. This same roster of Kemplin's company also lists Samuel Brady (the brother of John Brady) as a ranger (Section 7).

10. PA Archives, First Series, Vol. 12, "Daniel Brodhead's Letter Book, No. 2: to President Reed, April 15th, 1779", 106-108.
11. R. Swartz, "Ranger Groups of the Pennsylvania Frontier During the American Revolution, 1967, 60.
12. R. Swartz, "Ranger Groups....", 60.
13. George Roush, 19th Century Pension Papers in Richard B. LaCrosse, Jr., *The Frontier Rifleman*, 70-71.

14. Swartz, "Ranger Groups...", 61-62.
15. PA Archives, First Series, 12, "Daniel Brodhead's Letter Book: No. 25, To General Washington, June 25, 1779", 132. The author assumes George Wilson is Nanowland's English name.
16. PA Archives, 132.
17. Louise Phelps Kellogg, *Frontier Advance on the Upper Ohio: 1778-1779,* Footnote 1, 300.
18. Snyder, 304-305.
19. Snyder, 234.
20. Robert Emerson, *Fort Roberdeau: The Garrison and Military Life, 1778-1780,* 20.
21. Emerson, Appendix III, "Pension Records: Luke Tipton", 49-50.
22. Emerson, 49; 23.
23. Swartz, 39-40.
24. J. Niles Hubbard, *Sketches of Border Adventures in the Life and Times of Major Moses Van Campen,* 200.
25. Emerson, 34.
26. Emerson, 49.
27. Swartz, 42. As of this time, the author does not know the pay scale of the commissioned officers. The Colonial Records are nonspecific; the fiscal records of the County Lieutenants contained in the PA Archives, Third Series, Vol. 7, do not present any itemized breakdown.
28. Swartz, 46.
29. Swartz, 47-48.
30. PA Colonial Records, Vol. 12, "Minutes of the Supreme Executive Council, April 8, 1780", 311.
31. Swartz, 42-43.
32. Swartz, Chapter 5, 36-54.
33. Those that did should be honored. There is but one memorial to the Pennsylvania ranger, the Phillips Memorial near Saxton, PA. It was started by American Legion Post 169 in 1933, to honor those slain in battle near and tortured at the memorial's site. In 1957, the site was designated a responsibility of the Pennsylvania Historical and Museum Commission. (Jon Baughman, *Phillip's Rangers,* 31.)

Footnotes: Section 8

1. Floyd G. Hoenstein, *Soldiers of Blair County, Pennsylvania*, 22.
2. The horrific torture of Thomas Boyd and another prisoner is outlined in Graymont (Bibliography). It is as if the Iroquois were venting their full rage over the destruction of their nation on two bodies.
3. William Marion Schnure, "Northumberland County's Original Members of the Society of the Cincinnati", in: Charles F. Snyder, ed., *Northumberland County in the American Revolution*, 437-438.
4. Hoenstein, 31.
5. Hoenstein, 24.
6. (1) Robert L. Emerson, "Debacle on the Juniata: The Battle of Frankstown: 1781," *The Mansion*, 1. (2) PA Archives, First Series, Vol. 9, "George Ashman to President Reed, *Bedford County (Pennsylvania) in the American Revolution*, 44. Ashman at this time was County Lieutentant, Bedford County. U.J. Jones, in his History of the Early Settlement of the Juniata Valley, lists Captain Boyd and Lieutenant Harry Woods accompanied by eight rangers (see narrative).
7. Hoenstein, 23.
8. (1) James B. Whisker, "Alphabetical Listing, Bedford County Soldiers" (compiled from the Pennsylvania Archives) and "Original documents" in Orphan's Court Records, Bedford County Court House (including certificates signed by Captain John Boyd and Lieutenant George Smith), 58-A-136; 146. (2) Hoenstein, 24.
9. (1) U.J. Jones, *History of the Early Settlement of the Juniata Valley*, 307. (2) George H. Harris, "The Life of Horatio Jones," in Frank H. Severance, ed., *Publications of the Buffalo Historical Socidty*, Vol. 6, 393. The Jones listing is also cited by Hoenstein, 24, though Hoenstein cites as the Hollidays Captain John Holliday and perhaps his brother William; as the Colemans, Thomas and Michael, thus agreeing with Harris.
10. Hoenstein, 24
11. Whisker, 77.
12. Whisker, 77 (See cited sources of Whiskers, footnote 8).
13. E. Cruikshank, *Butler's Rangers*, 92.
14. Emerson, 1. The author believes this was most likely the Frankstown

	Branch of the Juniata River.
15.	Jones, 305.
16.	Jones, 305. The author believes this was most likely the Beaverdam Branch of the Juniata River.
17.	Emerson, 1.
18.	Hoenstein, p.1
19.	Harris, 394; Jones, 307.
20.	Harris, 387-389.
21.	Jones, 306. The Kittanning Path is the local name for the site of the major Indian Path from Harris' Ferry (Harrisburg) to Kittanning. From the present Hollidaysburg, the western portion of the path known by this name Kittanning Path. (See Wallace, *Indian Paths of Pennsylvania*, Bibliography.)
22.	Jones, 306-307. Harris, "Life of Horatio Jones", states that the two scouts reported the Indian encampment at Hart's Log. This is the opposite direction from Hart's Sleeping Place. (See map, Figure 10.1, Section 10.) Both places existed on the Frankstown Path. The complex trail system through Central Pennsylvania and the route taken by the raiding party make it logical for the location of this encampment to be Hart's Log (now Alexandria, PA). If the settlers were driven out, as many were by this time of the war, this area could have been abandoned. In terms of the route taken home, with prisoners (Section 11), Hart's Log makes sense as the site. However, in terms of the reports of the events and the other natural sites mentioned in the sources - such as Kittanning Gap, the mountains, etc., Hart's Sleeping Place makes sense as the site of the encampment. (For further discussion, see footnotes 13 and 15, Section 9.)

Footnotes: Section 9

1. George Harris, "The Life of Horatio Jones", in Frank H. Severance, ed, *Publications of the Buffalo Historical Society*, Vol. 6, 390-91.
2. Harris, 391.
3. Harris, 391-392.
4. E. Cruikshank, *Butler's Rangers*, 92.
5. Harris, 390.
6. U.J. Jones, *History of the Early Settlement of the Juniata Valley*, 308.
7. Jones, 308.
8. Harris, 390.
9. Harris, 392.
10. Harris, 392.
11. George P. Donehoo, *A History of the Indian Villages and Place Names in Pennsylvania*, 99-100. There is some discrepancy as to which creek was used: Pine or Lycoming. Tiadachton was also on of the Pennsylvania boundary lines for the 1768 treaty with the Iroquois at Ft. Stanwix which established Indian lands and white lands. Pennsylvania's colonial government officially disallowed settlement in Indian lands established by this treaty. Specifically, it did not recognize settlements in lands west of Lycoming Creek and north of the Susquehanna. Given these facts, a strong case can be made that colonial Pennsylvania recognized Lycoming Creek as Tiadachton.
12. Donehoo, 141-143.
13. Harris, 392. The general location of this camp is dependent upon where the advanced Indian encampment was: Hart's Log or Hart's Sleeping Place, both on the Frankstown Path. See Footnote 15, below. It was this advanced camp that was discovered by Boyd's scouts. (Section 8)
14. Harris, 392. The author believes that most likely this was the Frankstown Branch of the Juniata River.
15. Harris, 392. The pros and cons for Hart's Log or Hart's Sleeping Place as the advanced camps are summarized as follows. This writer leans toward the latter as the site of the advanced camp discovered by Boyd's scouts, though the proof is not conclusive.

Hart's Log - Pro

1. Logistically, the site of Hart's Log makes it easier to fulfill the mission.

2. Sources mention that Shongo moves down the Juniata and back up to join Hutson. barrier easity patrolled to This narrative supports a site along the river.

3. Hart's Log is in a more direct line of march to the Juniata settlements from the line of march that Harris describes; and the line of return.

4. Given the amount of raids, any settlement existing at Hart's Log could have been abandoned by the spring of 1781.

5. Via Indian paths, Hart's Log is 2 days from Bedford, from which Harris places the base camp.

Hart's Sleeping Place - Pro

1. This site fits the narrative and corroborated events in terms of terrain. The mountains to the east provide a safety barrier easily patrolled to guard against ambush.

2. Cross country, any base camp to the east or north might be 2 days from Bedford.

3. Boyd intended to meet the raiders before they got into the settlements.

4. Jones (Bibliography), a local historian, mentions this as the site.

5. Perhaps Shongo's moving down and back up the river refers to the Beaverdam Branch of the river and not the main fork. This could be done from Hart's Sleeping Place. Harris states this site was chosen.

6. An ambush site was chosen along the river. This

could also refer to the Beaverdam Branch. There is no controversy existing among sources as to where the ambush took place.

Hart's Log: Con

1. Even with lack of settlement, this site is risky in terms of sighting by patrols - militia or ranger.

2. Harris (Footnote 1) mentions this as the site. However, Harris was a New York historian and could have been confused about local designations.

Hart's Sleeping Place: Con

1. It is not in direct line of march, given Harris' description of the route taken to or from the Juniata, nor on any known northeast to southwest Indian trails.

16. Harris, 392. The author believes this is the Beaverdam Branch of the Juniata. The author also believes that Harris mistook Fetter's Fort for the Frankstown Blockhouse. Hence the phrase, "to watch the garrison at Fetter's", really refers to the blockhouse.

Footnotes: Section 10

1. Paul A.W. Wallace, *Indian Paths of Pennsylvania*, 51.
2. Wallace, 51.
3. Wallace, 51. Kittanning was to have been the site of the rendevous in April, 1778, between Tory instigators and at least 31 Bedford County Tories led by John Weston. Apparently the Bedford County contingent was to rendevous with the Indians and others, then invade the settlements in Bedford County. At Kittanning, the British-allied Indians mistook these men for invaders, fired upon them, and killed John Weston. Dispirited, the survivors fled back to Bedford County and the south. (See PA Archives, First Series,Vol. 6, "Examination of Richard Weston 1778", 542-543. See also, U.J. Jones, *History of the Early Settlement of the Juniata Valley* (H.A. Ashmead:np), 1856, 232-239.
4. Wallace, 51. Wallace here cites Hoenstein as saying Brush Creek. Swartz feels this should read Brush Run. Brush Creek and Brush Run are both existing today. Brush Creek is found east of Brush Run.
5. George P. Donehoo, *Indian Villages and Place Names in Pennsylvania*, 10.
6. Wallace, 51.
7. Wallace, 52.
8. Wallace, 52.
9. George H. Harris, "The Life of Horatio Jones,", in Frank H. Severance, ed., *Publications of the Buffalo Historical Society*, Vol. 6, 392.
10. Jones, 307. Knapsacks were different from haversacks. This is the only historian specifically alluding to knapsacks, which had two shoulder straps; the haversack, one, slung over the shoulder. The haversack was used for food rations; the knapsack, for equipment and personal belongings. (R.B. LaCrosse, Jr. *The Frontier Rifleman*, 162.) Perhaps a food bag might also be placed in a knapsack. A man would probably not carry both at the same time. A knapsack distributed weight more evenly, and a blanket could be stuffed between its two sides and thus carried, freeing the arms and shoulders. If a man placed a packed knapsack on first, and the canteen, powder horn, and hunting bag on last, the knapsack straps would not interfere with the

others' straps, thus providing more range of motion in use of these pieces of equipment. However, in surprise battle, such an arrangement caused dead weight. Any man would have to take off the horn, hunting bag, canteen, etc., to discard the pack.

11. Harris, 393-394. The reader will note that the type of dress worn by Butler's Rangers and PA rangers and frontier militia were very similar, except for insignia.
12. (1) Floyd Hoenstein, *Soldiers of Blair County, Pennsylvania,* 24; (2) R. Emerson, "Debacle on the Juniata: The Battle of Frankstown, 1781", *The Mansion,* Vol. 8, No. 2, June, 1981, 24.
13. Emerson, 2.
14. Harris, 394.
15. Hoenstein, 24.
16. Hoenstein, 24.
17. Hoenstein, 24.
18. Jones, 307.
19. Harris, 395-397; 405.
20. Jones, 308-309.
21. Jones, 309.
22. Jones, 307-308.
23. Jones, 308.
24. Hoenstein, 25. This story has not been substantiated, in terms of found remains. However, it is a fact that Henry was killed in this battle. See casualty figures listed in this section.
25. J.F. Meginness, *Otzinachson: A History of the West Branch Valley,* 660.
26. (1) E. Cruikshank, *Butler's Rangers,* 92. There is no indication to date as to differentiation between rangers and Iroquois - or the cause of casualties: rifle or musket fire or hand-to-hand combat.
    (2) M. Fryer, *The King's Men,* 164, reports the same casualties.
27. PA Archives, First Series, Vol. 9, "George Ashman to President Reed, 1781", 202-203, in: James B. Whisker, *Bedford County (Pennsylvania) in the American Revolution,* 44.
28. Hoenstein, 82.
29. PA Archives, in Whisker, 44.
30. Harris, 397.

31. R. Swartz, "Fort Muncy in the American Revolution", *Now and Then Magazine,* Vol. 24, No. 2, August 1994, 28-47.
32. Emerson, 1.
33. PA Archives, First Series, Vol. 9, "George Ashman to President Reed, 1781", 202-203, in: Whisker, 44.
34. Harris, 397.
35. Jones, 308.
36. See Whisker and Hoenstein, Bibliography, for example.
37. Hoenstein, 25. Hoenstein makes no reference as to how he collected or ascertained this listing. Volunteers may not have been privates in *any* military unit. Jones, 308, lists 17 killed in all.
39. Jones, 309.
40. Jones, 309.

Footnotes: Section 11

1. Floyd G. Hoenstein, *Soldiers of Blair County, Pennsylvania*, 25-26.
2. PA Archives, First Series, Vol. 9, "George Ashman to President Reed, 1781", 202-203, in: James B. Whisker, *Bedford County (Pennsylvania) in the American Revolution*, 44. One wonders how many volunteers could have been gathered together, given the enlistments of the Cumberland County militia being about to expire (Section 8). Was the lack of pursuit also due to the success of the raiders rather than simply high waters?
3. Whisker, 44.
4. Hoenstein, 25.
5. George H. Harris, "The Life of Horatio Jones", in Frank H. Severance, ed., *Publications of the Buffalo Historical Society*, 398.
6. Harris, 398.
7. Harris, 403.
8. Harris, 399.
9. Harris, 399. Most likely these would be Northumberland County militia and/or Captain Thomas Robinson's Rangers, who by this time in the Revolution had primary responsibility for Northumberland County defense. From headquarters at Fort Muncy, they patrolled both the North Branch and the West Branch of the Susquehanna, at least as far west as the Sinnemahoning Creek. Their overall lieutenant, Moses Van Campen, already had won a reputation among the Iroquois: they hated his guts figuratively and probably wanted them literally. Northumberland County, organized in 1772 politically encompassed the draining area of Bald Eagle Creek.

The author has discovered that at least two other events happened at Sinnemahoning, both of these being ambushes instigated by volunteers and/or rangers from Northumberland County against war parties. Both these were successful from the standpoint of the patriots. One of those involved was Moses Van Campen (see text). The author has not discovered if any loyalist rangers were involved. One of these incidents involved four men led by Peter Grove. The site of this ambush (which the author has visited) was the mouth of Grove Run in the present village of Sinnemahoning. The author firmly believes that the Grove ambush and the Van Campen ambush were two separate and distinct incidents. The Grove ambush occurred late summer, early autumn 1780 (Meginness, *Otzinachson, A History of the West Branch Valley*, 661-664). Meginness cites a state treasurer's report for September 30, 1780, paying these men ℒ1,875 for two Indian scalps (Meginness, 663).

The author places the Van Campen incident as separate, occurring in the summer of 1781. Van Campen describes this in his "Narrative of the Pennsylvania Frontier of Lieut. Moses Van Campen, During the War of the Revolution" (*Sunbury Gazette and Miners' Register*, Saturday, November 17, 1838). On first appearance, because it involves some of the same men and the same area, and because it occurred after the Grove ambush, it seems as if Van Campen might be "taking credit where it wasn't due". However, his commander, Capt. Thomas Robinson, Robinson's Rangers, writes in September of 1781: "Lieutenant Van Campen and six men have gone up into the Indian country, to discover their moves" (John Blair Linn, *Annals of Buffalo Valley*, 207). Van Campen's own words in his narrative allude to " discover": "We carried with us three weeks provisions, and proceeded up the West Branch with much caution and care; we reached the Sinnemahoning, but made no discovery except old tracks, we marched up the Sinnemahoning so far that we were satisfied it was a false report. [He had been sent to reconnoitre by Samuel Hunter, Lt. Col., Northumberland County, he states earlier.] We returned, and a little below Sinnemahoning near night we discovered smoke; we were confident it was a party of Indians, which we must have passed by or they got there some other way; we discovered there was a large party, how many we could not tell, but prepared for the attack..."

The Grove party was trailing the same raiding party all the way from Buffalo Valley, Northumberland County. The Van Campen patrol was sent to reconnoitre and discovered a raiding party. Thus the purposes of the two ambushes were different. This is another reason to regard the incidents as separate, besides Robinson's corroborating statement. If one travels from the site of Fort Muncy, headquarters for Robinson's Rangers, to Sinnemahoning, certainly one is going "up" in terms of elevation.

If Hart's Sleeping Place was the advanced camp (Section 9), the base camp would have been west or north of it, near the Kittanning Path. It is this path west that was probably taken by Nelles after the battle. To reach the Sinnemahoning and to avoid being on the West Branch of the Susquehanna night march probably was overland from the Kittanning Path, in a direct northeast direction. There are/were no known paths in the area.

10. Harris, 399. The fact that no gun was fired and no hunting was allowed indicated that bows and arrows were not used as weapons or for hunting.
11. Harris, 399.
12. Meginness, 660. There is no Ross listed with the lists of men known to have served or probably served at Frankstown. See Section 8 for listings.
13. Meginness, 660.
14. Meginness, 660-661.
15. Recall from Section 8 that Boyd's brother, Thomas, was horribly tortured to death in the Sullivan expedition..

The reader is encouraged to review Section 4 and elaboration contained in footnote 25, Section 4, for explanation of torture of prisoners.

This author believes Boyd was spared/adopted in this specific instance for two reasons - either one of which may be right. These are:
(1) Boyd was perceived by this woman, and perhaps by the warriors (another reason they did not interfere), as manifesting his power over them as he sang (See footnote 25, Section 4).
(2) As implausible as it seems, the woman recognized the Masonic song. The area about the Sinnemahoning is rife with hieroglyphs, some of which the author has viewed. These are similar to those found in ancient Europe, the Far East, and are the same symbols used

in Free Masonry. Joseph Brant, the Mohawk War chief, was a Mason, having joined a Masonic Lodge in London in 1776 (Isabel Thompson Kelsay, *Joseph Brant, 1743-1807: Man of Two Worlds*, 172). He also actively initiated one of the earliest Masonic Lodges in Upper Canada in 1797 (Kelsay, 536). How widespread were the beliefs of Free Masonry among the Iroquois? Is it possible that the natural symbols used in Masonry appealed to the Native American's traditional views of religion: God permeates nature?

16. Harris, 404-405.
17. Harris, 406-408. The village of Caneadea had a council house built by carpenters from Fort Niagara in 1780, similar to one described in this section's subsequent narrative (See Hubbard, Bibliography).
However, since the party was on the east bank of the Genesee and crossed the river to this village, it couldn't have been Caneadea, since this village stood on the east bank.
18. Harris, 405.
19. Harris, 408, 409.
20. Harris, 409-411,
21. Harris, 412-413.
22. (Harris, 413-414.) The torturing of the prisoners along the route, to the gauntlet and the fiendish fury of the warriors, drunk or sober, led by Wolf and Sharp Shins - might be an indication of the resistance offered by Boyd's men at the Beaverdam, especially considering Hutson's words.
23. Harris, 414.
24. J. Niles Hubbard, *Sketches of Border Adventures in the Life and Times of Major Moses Van Campen*, 222-229.
25. Harris 499; 500; 503-512.
26. Harris, 464.
27. Harris, 500-502.
28. Harris, 414-415.
29. Meginness, 661.
30. Meginness, 661. It is unfortunate that the names of the Iroquois women who saved Boyd's and Jones' lives are not preserved in history. Perhaps it is enough that the deeds are recorded for posterity in Heaven.

BIBLIOGRAPHY

Abbreviations used in this reference section:
    MSS: manuscript(s)
    np: no publisher *or* no place
    nd: no date
    nn: no number
    nv: no volume

A. Primary Sources

"Commissioners to Gen. Edward Hand", Transcript 3NN21-23, Draper MSS in: Thwaites, R.G., LL.D., and Kellogg, L.P., Ph.D. *Frontier Defense on the Upper Ohio, 1777-1778* .(Wisconsin Historical Society: Madison, WI), 1912, 238-240.

Doddridge, J. *Notes on the Settlement and Indian Wars of the Western Parts of Virginia and Pennsylvania from 1763 to 1783, inclusive...* Reprints: (1) (Ritenour & Lindsey: Pittsburgh, PA), 1912. (2) (McClain Printing Company: Parsons, WV), 1989.

"Extract from the Minutes of Congress, 25th Feb'y, 1778"; and "Extract from the Minutes of the General Assembly of Pennsylvania: March 29, 1779" in: "Pension Declarations for Revolutionary Service in Columbia County: Moses Van Campen" *Journals of the Works Progress Administration,* (Vol. 66, No. 3), Library, Northumberland County Historical Society, Sunbury, PA.

Hubbard, J.N. *Sketches of Border Adventures in the Life and Times of Major Moses Van Campen.* (np:np), 1842. Reprints: (1) second edition (np: Fillmore, NY), 1893. (2) (Zebrowski Historical Services and Publishing Company: Jersey Shore, PA), 1992. (*Author's note*: this company is now located in Middletown, NY. 1-800-753-3727.)

"McDonell to Butler, Tioga Point, Aug. 5th, 1779" Haldimand Papers, National Archives of Canada, MG 21, Add. Mss. 21760, (B-100), 223-225 (on reel H-1446).

Pennsylvania Colonial Records, Vol. 12.

Pennsylvania Archives, First Series, Vol. 2; 6; 7; 8; 12 (incl. "Daniel Brodhead's Letter Book").

Pennsylvania Archives, Second Series, Vol. 3; 14.

Pennsylvania Archives, Third Series, Vol. 7; 23.

"Recollections of Daniel Higgins", transcript 3S128-29, Draper MSS; and "Recollections of Captain Matthew Jack", transcript 6NN188, Draper MSS, in Kellogg, L.P., *Frontier Retreat on the Upper Ohio, 1779-1781*. (Wisconsin Historical Society: Madison, WI), 1917. Reprint: (Heritage Books, Inc., Bowie, MD), 1994, 59-61.

Rogers, R., Major. *Journals of Major Robert Rogers*. (J. Millan, Bookseller: Whitehall, London), 1765. Reprint: (Readex Microprint Corp.: US), 1966.

Seaver, J.E. *The Life of Mary Jemison: Deh-he-wa-mis*. (np: Pembroke, np), 1824. Reprint: (Zebrowski: Historical Services and Publishing Company: Jersey Shore, PA), 1991. (See *"Author's note"* in Hubbard reference, *Primary Sources*.)

Van Campen, M. "A Narrative of the Pennsylvania Frontier of Lieut. Moses Van Campen, During the War of the Revolution, 1777-1783", *Sunbury Gazette and Miners' Register*. (Vol. 1, No. 28), Saturday, November 17, 1838, in : Vol..15, *Works Progress Administration Journals*, at: Library, Northumberland County Historical Society, Fort Augusta Museum, Sunbury, PA.

B. Secondary Sources

1. *Books:*

Alden, J.R. *The American Revolution.* (Harper & Row: NY), 1954.

Africa, J.S. *History of Huntingdon and Blair Counties, Pennsylvania.* (Louis H. Everts: Philadelphia, PA), 1883. Reprint: (Huntingdon County Historical Society: Huntingdon, PA), 1990.

Bakeless, J. *Turncoats, Traitors and Heroes.* (J.B. Lippencott: NY), 1959.

Baughman, J. *Phillips' Rangers.* (Bedford County Press: Everett, PA), 1991.

Clarke, W.B. "Chapter II: Laws of the Revolutionary Period, 1775-1803", *Official History of the Militia and National Guard.* (Capt. Charles S. Hendler: np), 1909.

Craine, E.R. *The Story of Fort Roberdeau.* (Chamber of Commerce, City of Altoona: Altoona, PA), 1991.

Cruikshank, J. *Butler's Rangers and the Settlement of Niagara.* (Tribune Printing House: Welland, Ontario), 1893. Reprint: (Lundy's Lane Historical Society: Niagara Falls, Ontario), 1988.

Donehoo, G.P. *Indian Villages and Place Names in Pennsylvania.* (np: Harrisburg, PA), 1928. Reprint: (S.H. Horne/Pennsylvania Historical and Museum Commission/Gateway Press Place, Inc: Baltimore, MD), 1977.

Dowd, G.E. *"Power", A Spirited Resistance: The North American Indian Struggle for Unity, 1745-1815.* (Johns Hopkins Univ. Press: Baltimore), 1992, 1-22.

Eckert, A.W. *A Sorrow in Our Heart: the Life of Tecumseh.* (Bantam: NY), 1992.

Emerson, R. *Fort Roberdeau: The Garrison and Military Life, 1778-1780*, 2nd ed. (Fort Roberdeau Association: Altoona, PA), 1985.

Every, D.V. *A Company of Heroes: The American Frontier, 1775-1783.* (William Morrow and Company, Inc.: NY), 1962.

Fryer, M.B. *King's Men: the Soldier Founders of Ontario.* (Dundurn Press Limited: Toronto), 1980.

Graymont, B. *The Iroquois in the American Revolution.* (Syracuse University Press: Syracuse, NY), 1972.

Hoenstine, F.G. *Military Services and Genealogical Records of Soldiers of Blair County, Pennsylvania.* (Telegraph Press: Harrisburg, PA), 1940.

Jones, U. J. *History of the Early Settlement of the Juniata Valley.* (H.B. Ashmead: Philadelphia, PA), 1856. (*Author's note:* This work has been republished. Contact Fort Roberdeau Historic Site, Altoona, PA for further references.)

Kellogg, L.P. *Frontier Retreat on the Upper Ohio, 1779-1781.* (Wisconsin Historical Society: Madison, WI), 1917. Reprint: (Heritage Books, Inc., Bowie, MD), 1994, 55-66; 95-96.

Kelsay, I.T. *Joseph Brant, 1743-1807, Man of Two Worlds.* (Syracuse University Press: Syracuse, NY), 1984.

LaCrosse, R.B., Jr. *The Frontier Rifleman: His Arms, Clothing, and Equipment During the Era of the American Revolution, 1760-1800.* (Pioneer Press: Union City, TN), 1989.

Linn, J.B. "1781", *Annals of Buffalo Valley, Pennsylvania, 1755-1855.* (Lane S. Hart: Harrisburg, PA), 1877, 193-209. Reprint: Heritage Books, Inc., Bowie, MD, 1989.

Mathews, H.C. *The Mark of Honour.* (University of Toronto Press: Toronto), 1965.

Meginness, J.F. *Otzinachson: A History of the West Branch Valley of the Susquehanna, 2nd ed.* (np: Williamsport, PA), 1889. Reprint: (Lycoming County Historical Society, Williamsport, PA./Gateway Press, Inc.: Baltimore, MD), 1991

Montgomery, T.S., ed. *Report of the Commission to Locate the Site of the Frontier Forts of Pennsylvania,* 2nd ed., Volumes I & II. (Wm. Stanley Ray, State Printer: Harrisburg, PA), 1916.

Rossbacher, R.I. "Chapter 12: Facing the Second Front", *Now Remembered: Living Pennsylvania History Through 1900.* (University Press of America, Inc.: Lanham, MD), 1987.

Severance, F.H., ed. *Publications of the Buffalo Historical Society.* Vol. 6. (Buffalo Historical Society: Buffalo, NY), 1903.

Snyder, C.F., ed. *Northumberland County in the American Revolution.* (Northumberland County Historical Society: Sunbury, PA), 1976.

Thwaites, R.G., LL.D., and Kellogg, L.P., Ph.D. *Frontier Defense on the Upper Ohio, 1777-1778.* (Wisconsin Historical Society: Madison, WI), 1912, fn 70, p. 198. Reprint: (Heritage Books, Inc., Bowie, MD), 1993.

Trussell, J.B.B., illus. by C.C. Dallas, Jr. *The Pennsylvania Line: Regimental Organization and Operations, 1775-1783,* 2nd edition. (Pennsylvania Historical and Museum Commission: Harrisburg, PA), 1993. Frontispiece.

J.A. Tuck, "The Iroquois Confederacy" in: *Reprints from Scientific American: New World Archaeology, Theoretical and Cultural Transformations*. (W.H.Freeman & Co.: San Francisco), 1971, 190-200.

Waldman, C. and Braun, M., illus. "Algonquian", *Encyclopedia of Native American Tribes*. (Facts on File Publications: New York), 1988, 7-12.

Wallace, A.F.C. *King of the Delawares: Teedyuscung, 1700-1763*. (Syracuse University Press: Syracuse, NY), 1990, 59-66; 238; 254-261.

Wallace, P.A.W. *Indian Paths in Pennsylvania*. (Pennsylvania Historical and Museum Commission: Harrisburg, PA), 1971.

Whisker, J. B. *Bedford County (Pennsylvania) in the American Revolution*. (Closson Press: Apollo, PA), 1985.

Whiton, S. *Elements of Interior Design and Decoration*. (J.B. Lippencott: Philadelphia, PA), 1951, 286-289.

2.   *Articles:*

R. Alexander, "Pennsylvania's Revolutionary Militia", *The Pennsylvania Magazine of History and Biography* (Vol. 49, No. 1), January, 1945, 15-25.

C. A. Casada, "18th Century Camouflage", *The Backwoodsman* (Vol. 14, No. 5), September-October, 1993, 47-49.

D. Elliott, "Otsiningo, an Example of an Eighteenth Century Settlement Pattern" in:Current Perspectives in Northeastern Archeology: Essays in Honor of William A. Ritchie, R.E. Funk & C.F. Hayes III, ed. *Researches and Transactions of the New York Archaeological Association* (Vol.17, No.1), 1977, 93-105.

R. Emerson, "Debacle on the Juniata: the Battle of Frankstown, 1781", *The Mansion* (Vol. 8, No. 2), June, 1981, 1-2. (*Author's note: The Mansion* is the published bulletin of the Blair County Historical Society, Altoona, PA.)

L. Fossler, "Samuel Wallis: Colonial Merchant, Secret Agent", *Proceedings of the Northumberland County Historical Society* (Vol. 30, nn), December 10, 1990, 107-115. *(Author's note:* The Northumberland County Historical Society is located at Fort Augusta Museum, Sunbury, PA.)

P.P. Pratt, "A Perspective on Oneida Archeology" in Current Perspectives of Northeastern Archeology: Essays in Honor of William A. Ritchie, R.E. Funk & C.F. Hayes III, ed., *Researches and Transactions of the New York Archeological Association* (Vol. 17, No.1), 1977, 51-69.

D.K. Richter, "War and Culture: The Iroquois Experience", *William and Mary Quarterly,* (Vol. 40, No. 3), 1983, 528-559.

R.G. Swartz, "Fort Muncy During the American Revolution", *Now and Then Magazine,* (Muncy Historical Society, Muncy, PA), (Vol. 24, No. 2), August, 1994, 28-47.

R.G. Swartz, "Ranger Companies of the Pennsylvania Frontier and Northumberland County During the American Revolution", *Now and Then Magazine (Muncy Historical Society),* (Vol. 23, No. 10), April, 1993, 243-250.

3. *Other:*

Joseph R. Fisher. *A Well Executed Failure: The Sullivan Campaign Against the Iroquois, July-September, 1779.* A thesis in history submitted in partial fulfillment of the requirements for the degree of Doctor of Philosophy, Pennsylvania State University, March, 1993. *(Author's note:* This work is available for study at the library of the Northumberland County Historical Society, Fort Augusta Museum, Sunbury, PA.)

"The Military System of Pennsylvania During the Revolutionary War," *Information Leaflet No. 3.* (Pennsylvania Historical and Museum Commission:

Harrisburg, PA), 1969, 1-4.

     R.G. Swartz. *Ranger Groups of the Pennsylvania Frontier During the American Revolution,* 1967. A thesis submitted in partial requirement for both the History Department (required: Master level thesis) and for the Bachelor of Arts degree, Albright College. *(Author's notes:* The thesis is on file at the library, Albright College, Reading, PA. This thesis was recognized in 1967 as the best thesis, senior class, by the local chapter of the Phi Alpha Theta National Honorary History Society.)

Notes:

Notes:

Notes:

ABOUT THE AUTHOR
Roger Swartz,
B.A., M.A. Ed., M.P.A.

The author at Fort Freeland during Heritage Society Days, Oct. 2, 1994.
(Photograph by T. Laru Moyer of Muncy, PA.)

The author graduated from Albright College (Reading, PA) in 1967, majoring in history. Since then, he has authored *Accelerated Learning: **How** You Learn Determines **What** You Learn* (Essential Medical Information Systems: Durant, OK), 1991; and co-authored (with Gretchen Peske, M.S., R.N.) *Your Dollars, Your Health: Healing Strategies and Skills* (Blue Path Press: Hockessin, DE), 1995. The former has received plaudits in two national reviews: the *American Society for Training and Development Journal* (May, 1992) and the national newsletter of the American Society for Healthcare Education and Training (January, 1993). His self-published workbook, *Music to Learn by: Self-Accelerated Learning Skills* (2nd ed., R.G. Swartz & Associates: Lancaster, PA 1990), received international acclaim in the United Kingdom's *Training and Development Journal* (November, 1992).

Mr. Swartz has been contributing editor for *Now and Then*, the magazine of the Muncy Historical Society (Muncy, PA). He and his associates conduct workshops related to the content of this book for school districts, historical organizations, and colleges. In addition, he is a re-enactor, portraying a frontier ranger during the American Revolution.

His business, R.G. Swartz & Associates, also specializes in the application of accelerated learning skills to education, workforce staff development, and personal growth - especially for the healing process.

Mr. Swartz holds two Master degrees from Lehigh University.